NO PLOT? NO PROBLEM!

A Low-Stress,
      High-Velocity Guide
to Writing a Novel
      in 30 Days

Chris Baty
FOUNDER OF NATIONAL NOVEL WRITING MONTH

CHRONICLE BOOKS
SAN FRANCISCO

Library of Congress Cataloging-in-Publication Data available.

ISBN 0-8118-4505-2

Manufactured in Canada.

Design by Charles Wilkin/Automatic

Distributed in Canada by Raincoast Books
9050 Shaughnessy Street
Vancouver, British Columbia V6P 6E5

10 9 8 7 6 5 4 3

Chronicle Books LLC
85 Second Street
San Francisco, California 94105

www.chroniclebooks.com

FOR MY PARENTS,

who knew

  it was possible

all along.

CONTENTS

SECTION TWO

Write Here! Write Now! A Frantic, Fantastic
Week-by-Week Overview to Bashing out Your Book

Introduction

The era, in retrospect, was very kind to dumb ideas.

The year was 1999, and I was working as a writer in the San Francisco Bay Area, drinking way too much coffee and watching the dot-com boom rewrite the rules of life around me.

Back then, it seemed entirely feasible—nay, inevitable—that my friends and I would spend three tiring years in the workforce, throwing nerf balls at each other and staging madcap office-chair races. And then we'd cash in our hard-earned stock options, buy a small island somewhere, and helicopter off into blissful retirement.

It was a delicious, surreal moment, and in the middle of it all I decided that what I really needed to do was write a novel in a month. Not because I had a great idea for a book. On the contrary, I had no ideas for a book.

All of this made perfect sense in 1999.

In a more grounded age, my novel-in-a-month concept would have been reality-checked right out of existence. Instead, the very first National Novel Writing Month set sail two weeks later, with almost everyone I knew in the Bay Area on board.

That the twenty-one of us who signed up for the escapade were undertalented goofballs who had no business flailing around at the serious endeavor of novel writing was pretty clear. We hadn't taken any creative writing courses in college, or read any how-to books on story or craft. And our combined post-elementary–school fiction output would have fit comfortably on a Post-it Note.

My only explanation for our cheeky ambition is this: Being surrounded by pet-supply e-tailers worth more than IBM has a way of getting your sense of what's possible all out of whack. The old millennium was dying; a better one was on its way. We were in our mid-twenties, and we had no idea what we were doing. But we knew we loved books. And so we set out to write them.

BOOKISH HOOLIGANS

That love of books, I think, was the saving grace of the whole enterprise. However unseriously we had agreed to take the writing process, we had an absolute reverence for novels themselves, the papery bricks of goodness that, once pried apart, unleashed the most amazing visions in their owners. In books, we'd found magical portals and steadfast companions, witnessed acts of true love and gaped at absolute evil. Books, as much as our friends and parents, had been our early educators, allowing us our first exciting glimpses into life beyond the gates of childhood.

If we loved books, we were equally awestruck by their creators. Novelists were clearly a different branch of Homo sapiens; an enlightened subspecies endowed with a monstrously overdeveloped understanding of the human condition and the supernatural ability to spell words properly.

Novelists, we knew, had it made. They got fawned over in book-stores, and were forever being pestered for insights on their genius in newspapers and magazines. They had license to dress horribly, wear decades-out-of-date hairstyles, and have their shortcomings interpreted as charming quirks and idiosyncrasies rather than social dysfunctions.

Best of all, novel writing was for them a lifetime sport, one of the few branches of the entertainment industry where you are allowed to have a career long after you've stopped looking good in hot pants.

In short, we adored novels and glorified writers, and thought that if, after a month's labors, we could claim even the thinnest of alliances with that world, something mysterious and transformational would happen to us. The possibility of starting the month with nada and ending it with a book we'd written—no matter how bad that book might be—was irresistible. And though we never admitted it to one another, there was also the hope that maybe, just maybe, we'd yank an undeniable work of genius from the depths of our imagina-tion. A masterpiece-in-the-rough that would forever change the liter-ary landscape. The Accidental American Novel. Just think of the acclaim! The feelings of satisfaction! The vastly increased dating opportunities!

The power this last point held over us, sadly, is not to be under-estimated. And as a music nerd, I *knew* it could happen. The annals of rock and roll are filled with self-taught musicians who recorded albums first and learned how to play an instrument much later. The Sex Pistols, the Ramones, Beat Happening—they were all inspirational examples of unpolished, untrained people who went from nobodies to kings and queens of their oeuvre through sheer exuberance.

If fantasies of screaming, headbanging fans forming mosh pits at our book signings were flitting through our minds in 1999, though, we weren't admitting it to anyone. Officially, this whole month-long novel-writing thing was to be an exercise in slapdash mediocrity. The more you wrote and the less you pretended to care, the better your standing in the field.

So at the dawn of the first National Novel Writing Month we laughed and toasted one another's complete lack of preparation and dismal chances of success with gusto. Much like novice sailors making good on a drunken dare, we were sailing out to sea on an already-sinking ship.

And that, on July 1, 1999, was how National Novel Writing Month began: Twenty-one of us waving merrily to well-wishers gathered on shore, blowing kisses at our friends and family as we secretly cast nervous glances around the deck for life rafts.

We had no idea at the time how soon we'd end up needing them.

A MONTH AT SEA

Writer and championship figure skater Ralph Waldo Emerson once wrote, "In skating over thin ice, our safety is in our speed." As we hurled ourselves toward our likely literary demise, we were nothing if not quick about it.

The opening week of NaNoWriMo (as we were all soon calling it) was an overcaffeinated typing frenzy. For the sake of clarity, we had all agreed to define a novel as 50,000 words of fiction. With that lofty goal in sight, quantity quickly took precedence over quality, and we met in coffeeshops after work each night to add another couple thousand words of girth to our literary creations.

As we wrote, we gave ourselves word quotas and created elaborate challenges and races. Anyone who hadn't reached their writing goal wasn't allowed to get drink refills or go to the bathroom until they hit the mark. It was ridiculous, screaming fun, and the levity of those early sessions infused what would have normally been a terrifying endeavor—writing a book in an absurdly short amount of time—into a raucous field trip to novel-land.

The rambunctious mood of those first few days was further buoyed by the fact that the writing campaign started off well for all of us. In short order, we had settings, main characters, and a few chapters under our belts. The hardest part was over, it seemed, and we settled into our novels with the happy assurance that our muses would ably guide us through whatever unfamiliar terrain lay ahead.

Our muses, it turned out, had other plans.

Becalmed

By the seven-day mark, the initial excitement had worn off, and it revealed a sad and ugly truth: Our novels were bad. Maybe even horrible. As Week One slipped away, the intoxicating speed of the escapade ground to a halt, and we began poking at our novels with the dismay of a third grader whose heaping portion of dessert has been swapped for a plate of mushy vegetables.

When we broached the subject of our flagging motivations during one of our writing sessions, it became clear that most of us were having the same problem: Starting had been easy. Continuing was hard. Perhaps flinging a random assortment of characters at a Microsoft Word document, we admitted, was not the soundest approach to book-building. And maybe trying to cram something as large as novel writing into an already busy schedule doomed both life and literature.

Our lives certainly had taken on the feel of cursed things: Giving over every free moment to one's novel meant no sleeping-in on weekends, no matinee movies, and no languorous dinners with friends. Instead, we spent our downtime prodding at lifeless characters and wondering how long a human body could subsist on an all-ramen and Coke diet before liver functions ceased entirely.

By the middle of Week Two, we were ready to mutiny. Half of the participants dropped out. Unfortunately, some of us had bragged so widely about our heroic novel-writing quest that we were too ashamed to quit before the month ended. So we slogged on, continuing to meet for less-than-joyous writing sessions. We were no longer in it to win it; our plan at that point was just to run out the clock.

Week Two came and went. And then some strange things started happening.

The aimless, anemic characters we'd invented in the first fourteen days began to perk up and *do* things. Quirky, unexpected, readable things. They sold their SUVs and started commuting to work in golf carts. They joined polka bands and got kidnapped by woodland creatures and found themselves organizing jewel-heist capers with their next-door neighbors from the nursing home.

It was as if our main characters, tired of waiting for competent stage direction from us, simply took control of the show. Thankfully, they turned out to be far better storytellers than we ever were.

The listlessness of Week Two lifted, and the flat lines of our novels began to resemble the trajectories of honest-to-God story arcs. We were still tired, sure. But our books had gone from being albatrosses around our necks to welcoming ports in the storm of everyday life. Rather than dreading the nightly drudgery of writing, we began fantasizing about what directions the story would take in the course of the evening's work. We called our answering machines to dictate plot breakthroughs we'd hatched on our morning commutes, and scribbled out ever-lengthening backstories on napkins, receipts, coworkers; anything we could get our hands on to capture some of the ideas that were pouring out of our overtaxed brains.

To be fair, the novels emerging on our hard drives were far from the works of genius we'd secretly hoped for. They were stiff and awkward creatures, riddled with enormous plot holes, their loose ends flopping lewdly. But they were beautiful in their own ungainly way. And absolutely breathtaking in their potential.

If You Build It,
Kevin Costner Will Come

Needless to say, at this point we were freaked out of our minds. It felt like we'd stumbled through a portal into a giddy netherworld, a Narnia for grown-ups where hours passed like seconds and the most outrageous and wonderful things you imagined became real.

It was one of the best, most fulfilling experiences of my life, and, sadly, the only thing I can compare it to is the movie *Field of Dreams*—where Kevin Costner, playing an Iowa farmer, begins hearing voices that tell him: *"If you build it, they will come."*

At the advice of the creepy voices, Kevin distances himself from his nay-saying wife and does what any self-respecting man would do: He wrecks his cornfield and builds a professional-grade baseball diamond next to his farmhouse. He's clearly berserk. Possessed. Crazy as a loon.

Those of us heading towards the fourth week of NaNoWriMo could relate.

In the movie, Costner's wacko labors are rewarded with the appearance of ghostly baseball greats from bygone eras, who play exhibition games and inspire epiphanies in James Earl Jones. For us, the rewards were similarly bountiful. After two weeks of tilling the meager, gravelly soil of our imaginations, the stories we'd been doggedly tending bloomed riotously. In Week Three, we harvested bumper crops of plot twists and fascinating characters, all of them eager to have their star turns on the sets we'd created.

Though undeniably lousy baseball players, they were good at other things. My characters, for example, were good at sleeping with people they weren't supposed to. Another person's characters were good at taking road trips. And someone else's were good at inventing fonts that, when viewed, made people's brains explode.

To each their own. Whatever varied directions our stories were moving in, they were definitely *moving*. And they were dragging us, happy and wide-eyed, in their wake.

On Day 29, the first participant crossed the 50,000-word finish line. Another followed. Then another. July came to a close, and as exhilarating as it had been to spend thirty-one days exploring the outer reaches of our imaginations, we were all ready to return to real life. So we wrapped up our stories, put our characters to bed, and turned out the lights one by one in the worlds we'd created.

Of the twenty-one people who participated, only six of us made it across the 50,000-word finish line that first year, with the rest falling short by anywhere from 500 to 49,000 words. Everyone who participated in the escapade, though, came away from the experience changed by it.

Some participants, to be honest, realized that they never wanted to write another book again. Others were ready to apply the next day to MFA programs in creative writing. For me, the revelation I couldn't shake was this: The biggest thing separating people from their artistic ambitions is not a lack of talent. It's the lack of a *deadline*. Give someone an enormous task, a supportive community, and a friendly-yet-firm due date, and miracles will happen.

Thanks to the go-go-go structure of the event, the stultifying pressure to write brilliant, eternal prose had been lifted. And in its place was the pleasure of learning by doing. Of taking risks, of making messes. Of following ideas just to see where they lead.

Writing for quantity rather than quality, I discovered, had the strange effect of bringing about both. It didn't necessarily make a whole lot of sense to me, especially as a writer who had spent days laboring over seventy-five-word record reviews for the local paper. But the proof was incontrovertible, and everyone who finished NaNoWriMo that first year agreed: We were only able to write so well—and have such a merry time doing it—because we wrote so quickly and intensely. The roar of adrenaline drowned out the self-critical voices that tend to make creative play such work for adults.

LESSONS LEARNED

I've organized National Novel Writing Month every year since 1999. I now have three books in various states of editorial redemption, along with two hopelessly execrable rough drafts whose highest calling in life will forever be propping up a listing leg of my couch. Through the good books and bad, I've learned a lot about getting first drafts written, and picked up countless strategies, tips, and housemate-annoying behaviors that help get that initial, breathless sketch of a novel down on paper.

I think the lasting lessons from that first year, though, boil down to just four revelations.

1) Enlightenment Is Overrated

Before being swept up in the momentum of National Novel Writing Month, my general approach to fiction writing was to stall as long as possible. In fact, I had high hopes of delaying any novel writing attempts until I was older and wiser, and had achieved a state of complete literary enlightenment.

From this position of all-seeing wisdom, I knew I would have amassed a roster of brilliant, original plots and dynamic, compelling characters. And then I could cherry-pick the best ones for my masterful creation.

If all went according to plan, I figured the state of enlightenment would descend on my bald head sometime around my ninetieth birthday. And then, fully primed, I could simply dictate the Nobel Prize–worthy manuscript to my assistant or nursemaid, who would then pass it on to an appropriate publisher.

Having written a not-irredeemable novel as a twenty-six-year- old made me realize that "sooner" definitely trumps "later" when it comes to writing. Every period in one's life, I saw, bustles with novel-worthy passions, dilemmas, and energies specific to that age. The novel I wrote at twenty-six is much different than the one I wrote at thirty, which will (hopefully) be much different than the one I write at fifty. What better reason to get writing now? With each passing era, a new novel is possible. And a potentially great book you could have written slips away into noveling oblivion.

2) Being Busy
Is Good for Your Writing

You've probably heard the old adage that if you want to get something done, you should ask a busy person to do it. I've discovered this is acutely true when it comes to novel writing.

Because here's the thing: However attractive the idea of a writer's retreat may sound, having all day to poke around on a novel actually *hampers* productivity. This is something I suspected after the first year of NaNoWriMo, and something I confirmed after the second—when, emboldened by a pair of questionable successes in the month-long noveling field, I decided that the only thing separating me from Oprah's Book Club was three months of uninterrupted writing time with my laptop.

And so I spent the following half year saving up enough money to resign my various obligations for three months, and then dove into the deliriously productive life of a full-time novelist.

Things went awry almost immediately. With nothing to do all day but write, I found myself doing everything *but* writing. Essential errands were run. Laundry was done. The bathroom was cleaned. Less essential errands were run. The bathroom was re-cleaned. A complex rooftop Habitrail system designed to make tree-to-tree transitioning easier for the neighborhood squirrels was built and nearly installed before the county's animal services unit intervened. And so on.

The mounting guilt I felt each evening over accomplishing so little writing during the day would then force me to cancel the plans

I had made with friends that night. So I could stay in and get some writing done.

Night, of course, simply involved more work on the Habitrail.

At the end of the three months, I was frustrated, my friends were worried, and the squirrels continued to make their clumsy, desperate leaps from branch to branch. The experiment in nonstop writing was a total disaster.

For me the moral of the story is this: A rough draft is best written in the steam-cooker of an already busy life. If you have a million things to do, adding item number 1,000,001 is not such a big deal. When, on the other hand, you have *nothing* to do, getting out of bed and washing yourself before 2:00 P.M. feels like too much work to even contemplate.

As Isaac Newton observed, objects in motion tend to stay in motion. When writing your first draft, being busy is key. It may feel frustrating at first, but having daily writing periods curtailed by chores, family, and other distractions actually *helps* you get the thing done. This is partly because the hectic pace forces you type with a fleet-fingered desperation. But it's mostly because noveling in the midst of a chaotic life makes "book time" a treat rather than an obligation. It's a small psychological shift, but it makes all the difference in the world.

3) Plot Happens

From that first NaNoWriMo, I learned that you are allowed to begin a novel simply by turning on the nearest computer and typing. You don't need to do research; you don't need to understand anything about your characters or plan out your setting. It's fine to just *start*. And making it up as you go along does not require you to be a particularly gifted novelist. That first year, I started with neither plot nor characters, and I ended up with a reasonably accomplished novel that had tension and momentum and even a subplot or two. And I did all that with an imagination the size of a pea.

If you spend enough time with your characters, plot simply happens. This makes novel writing, in essence, a literary trapeze act, one where you have to blindly trust that your imagination and intuition will be there to catch you and fling you onward at each stage of your high-flying journey.

The good news is that our imaginations *live* for these high-pressure situations. The human brain is an agile, sure-handed partner, an attention-loving, razzle-dazzle showthing that can pull plausible transitions out of thin air and catch us before anything (save our pride) gets too terribly injured on our inevitable tumbles.

The key to writing a novel is to realize that you are in the greatest hands possible: your own. Ray Bradbury said it best: "Your intuition knows what it wants to write, so get out of the way."

4) Writing for Its Own Sake
Has Surprising Rewards

That first year I learned that writing a novel simply *feels* great. Slipping into "the zone"—that place where you become a passive conduit to a story—exercises your brain in weird, pleasant ways and just makes life a little bit more enchanted. No matter what your talent level, novel writing is a low-stress, high-rewards hobby.

After I'd written my own manuscript, I also found myself able to appreciate my favorite books on a different level. I stopped taking the text for granted and began noticing a host of crafty details and well-concealed seams. To really get behind the scenes and understand the books you love as beautiful art *and* crafted artifice, it helps to write one yourself. Creating my own manuscript also opened my mind to the joys of genres I'd never read before, as I become curious about the way different kinds of books are constructed.

And finally, the more I wrote, the better my writing became. I now see each of the month-long novels I've written as a thirty-day scholarship to the most exclusive, important writing academy in the world. If there's one thing successful novelists agree on, it's this: The single best thing you can do to improve your writing is to write. Copiously.

The more books you have under your belt, the more comfortable you are with your writing voice, and the more confident you are in your style. Treating a novel like a hands-on writing classroom—where advancement relies as much on dramatic failures as it does on heroic successes—has been an amazingly liberating experience for me. And it's taught me exactly which aspects of noveling I'm good at (coffee drinking and complaining) and what my weaknesses are (dialogue, character development, plot, etc.).

It's invaluable feedback, and I couldn't have gotten it any other way.

MEANWHILE, BACK AT NANOWRIMO HEADQUARTERS

And what happened to NaNoWriMo after that first year? In 2000, I moved National Novel Writing Month from July to November to more fully take advantage of the miserable weather. That second year, an amazing 140 people signed up, and 29 people ended up winning.

Then word began to spread about NaNoWriMo. The *Los Angeles Times* did an article, as did *USA Today*. A talented engineer built the new, more-robust NaNoWriMo.org site for the event, one with discussion boards, novel-excerpt posting areas, personalized word-count progress bars, and a winner verification system.

The event grew larger still—five thousand participants the third year—and I continued to work as both director and participant, sending out pep-talk emails, overseeing the Web site, and interacting with nascent NaNoWriMo chapters around the world.

In November 2003, NaNoWriMo celebrated its fifth anniversary with more than twenty-five thousand participants from over thirty countries. By my calculations, NaNoWriMo is now responsible for more fiction each year than all of America's creative writing programs combined.

A handful of participants have gone on to edit and sell their creations to big-time publishing houses like Pinnacle and Warner Books. The biggest success stories of National Novel Writing Month, though, are rarely the published ones. These are the stories of everyday people who, over the course of one frantic month, discover that literature is not merely a spectator sport. Who discover that fiction writing can be a blast when you set aside debilitating notions of perfection and just dive headlong into the creative process.

YOUR MISSION

No Plot? No Problem! is intended as a guidebook and companion for that month-long vacation into the weird, wonderful realm of the imagination. In its nine chapters, I've tried to stuff five years of novel-writing tips, tricks, strategies, and schemes, as well as do's, don'ts, and encouraging anecdotes from dozens of NaNoWriMo veterans. Chapters one through three describe how to prepare for the actual writing month. They guide you in creating a realistic schedule and in gathering the tools and treats that are essential in bashing your book out. They also look at ways to turn your home and immediate surroundings into phenomenally productive word factories, and lay out winning tactics to transform innocent bystanders into cheerleaders and fellow travelers on the journey.

Chapter four introduces such novelish concepts as plot, setting, and character, and helps you uncover what it is you'd actually like to write about during your upcoming writing marathon.

Chapters five through eight serve as a week-by-week guide to your writing adventure. They lay out the issues and dilemmas particular to each week, and offer plenty of exercises for sparking your creativity and goofy ways to bag the day's word-count quota while maintaining inspired and generally coherent storytelling.

Chapter nine offers some thoughts and advice on post-novel life, particularly on making a graceful transition back into the day-to-day world, and it also contains a guide to rewriting one-month novels for those interested in shaping and polishing their work into publish-worthy form.

No Plot? No Problem! makes a perfect companion for those look-ing to undertake the madcap National Novel Writing Month in Novem-ber. But because November is an already-overloaded month for many people (students, I'm looking at you), *No Plot? No Problem!* was also created as a year-round personal trainer for anyone inter-ested in embarking on their own month-long noveling journey.

Whether you plan on writing your novel in winter or summer, next week or next year, I hope you'll find in these pages the friendly kick in the pants needed to help you take your book from embry-onic idea to completed draft in one action-packed month.

With great caffeinated well-wishes,

SECTION ONE

A Round-Trip Ticket
to Novel-land:
Gearing up for Your
Writing Adventure!

CHAPTER **1**

Secret Weapons,

    Exuberant Imperfections,

and the End of the

    "One Day" Novelist

Once upon a time, I believed that you needed to have several things before you set out to write a novel. These were, in order of importance:

1) Heart-fibrillating amounts of coffee

2) Plot

3) Character

4) Setting

When I actually sat down to write my first novel back in 1999, though, I discovered that my ideas about novel writing were woefully mistaken. You *don't* need a plot before you write a novel, nor do you need an evocative sense of place or a winsome, engaging cast. You don't even need coffee (though I still haven't allowed myself to fully come to terms with that yet).

What you really need is a secret weapon.

You need a superpowered, diabolical device that will transform you into a bastion of literary accomplishment. And I'm happy to report that this implement is in the house, and it's just waiting for you to pick it up.

THE MYSTERY MACHINE AND YOU

Without hyperbole, I can say that this tool (tucked securely at the end of this chapter) is the most awesome catalyst that has ever been unleashed on the worlds of art and commerce. Nearly every beautiful and useful thing you've ever touched or witnessed was born in its mighty forge. It's portable, affordable, and nonpolluting.

It's also invisible.

What you need to write a novel, of course, is a deadline.

Deadlines are the dynamos of the modern age. They've built every city, won every contest, and helped all of us pay our taxes reasonably close to on time for years and years. Deadlines bring focus, forcing us to make time for the achievements we would otherwise postpone, encouraging us to reach beyond our conservative estimates of what we think possible, helping us to wrench victory from the jaws of sleep.

A deadline is, simply put, optimism in its most ass-kicking form. It's a potent force that, when wielded with respect, will level any obstacle in its path. This is especially true when it comes to creative pursuits.

Because in the artistic realms, deadlines do much more than just get projects finished. They serve as creative midwives, as enthusiastic shepherds adept at plucking the timid inspirations that lurk in the wings of our imaginations and flinging them bodily into the bright light of day. The bigger the artistic project, the more it needs a deadline to keep marshaling those shy ideas out onto the world's stage.

Nowhere is this more true than in novel writing, when even people who know what they're doing have trouble getting the things finished. Drafting a novel typically involves years of navigating a jungle of plots, subplots, supporting characters, tangents, symbols, and motifs. It's an exhilarating trek at times, but it also involves long, long slogs, where chapters are built, dismantled, and rebuilt dozens of times. A single troublesome passage may stop the writing for years as the writer fusses and stews and waits for the way forward to become clear.

 THIS DANGEROUS BLOODSPORT CALLED NOVEL WRITING

If you've spent any amount of time using a computer, you already know the range of sneaky, bloodthirsty ways they have of wrecking your body. Carpal tunnel syndrome, eye strain, back problems, numb-butt...the list of computer-inspired woes goes on and on.

Because you'll likely be racking up an extraordinary amount of keyboard time when you write your novel, you are going to be putting your body at high risk for damage. This is no joke: Take it easy on yourself by setting up an ergonomic writing station, making a point of taking stretching breaks, and calling it a night at the first sign of numbness. Several companies, such as Workpace.com and Rsiguard.com, offer free one-month trials (woo hoo!) of software that will lock up your computer at intervals chosen by you, and then lead you through on-screen stretching exercises. Look on the Web for eye exercises as well, and keep some eye drops on hand to ward off the inevitable dryness that comes from getting so wrapped up in your book that you forget to blink (a great sign for your story, but a not-so-great sign for your poor eyeballs).

WHY BRINGING A PARTIALLY COMPLETED BOOK INTO THIS IS NOT SUCH A GOOD IDEA

In National Novel Writing Month, one of the fundamental rules of the game is that you must start your novel from scratch on Day One of the event. You can bring as many outlines and notes and character maps as you like, but writing any of the book's actual prose in advance is forbidden. This rule is enforced by legions of invisible guilt-monkeys, which are unleashed every year against those who dare to break the rules.

While this costs NaNoWriMo a pretty penny annually in guilt-monkeys, it also keeps things fresh and exciting and helps prevent people from sabotaging their productivity by being overly invested in the outcome of their book.

If your writing frenzy is taking place outside of the tyrannical bounds of NaNoWriMo, guilt-monkeys will not descend should you choose to spend the month adding 50,000 words to a novel you've already started. Be warned, though, that a state of exuberant imperfection is hard to attain when you've set yourself the formidable task of building a suitable extension onto an earlier creation. The writing will be slower, the pain much greater, and the output will likely leave you disappointed. My strong advice is to come up with something new for this challenge. You'll be happy you did.

Writing on deadline changes that. Having an end-date for your quest through the noveling unknown is like bringing along a team of jetpack-wearing, entrepreneurial Sherpas. These energetic guides not only make passage easier through myriad formidable obstacles, but they'll fly ahead and open coffeeshops and convenience stores along the route.

A Good Deadline Is Hard to Find

The problem, as those of us who are forever grumbling about our uncreative lives know, is that rock-solid, dream-fostering deadlines are hard to come by in the arts world. It's a sad irony that deadlines are given so freely at work (where we want them least), and are in such short supply in the extracurricular activities where we need them most.

Outside of writing classes, we never quite get the professional-grade push we need to tackle big, juicy, creative projects like novel writing. And who has time for classes? We're slammed at work and busy at home. Throw in an occasional outing with friends or significant others, and we're ready for bed at 10:00 P.M. every night. *Really* ready for bed. There's barely enough time in a day to cover all our mandatory obligations, so optional activities like novel writing, journaling, painting, or playing music—things that feel great but that no one will ever take us to task for shirking—are invariably left for another day.

Which is how most of us become "one day" novelists. As in, "One day, I'd really like to write a novel." The problem is that that day never seems to come, and so we're stuck. Or we *were* stuck, anyway. Because as far as artistic deadlines go, this book comes with a doozy.

The deadline that rules over this book with an iron fist is the ink-sensitive model #A30/31/50k. Once activated, it gives you just one month to write a 50,000-word rough draft of a novel. Plus, it hounds you every step of the way, forcing you to write when you don't want to, badgering you into meeting daily word-count goals, and turning your life into an obsessive literary hell for four weeks.

The #A30/31/50k will also foster one of the most intense and satisfying months of your life. In the thirty or thirty-one days you spend under its taskmastering thumb, you'll discover wild, wonderful parts of yourself and tap into exciting realms of aptitude and achievement you didn't know existed. You'll fly and soar and laugh and sing, and the people who love you most will likely worry that you've gone crazy.

That's okay. The insanity only lasts a month, just long enough to get "write a novel" checked off your to-do list. And then normal life, with its regular showers and reasonably clean apartments, can begin again. Should you decide to take your month-long novel and revise it to perfection later, you can do that. If not, you'll still have experienced a creative month like no other.

OKAY, ONE MONTH SOUNDS GOOD. BUT WHY 50,000 WORDS?

I'd like to say that NaNoWriMo's 50,000-word threshold was achieved by a scientific assessment of the great short novels of our age. The real story is that when I started this whole month-long noveling escapade five years ago, I simply grabbed the shortest novel on my shelf—which happened to be Aldous Huxley's *Brave New World*—did a rough word count of it, and went with that figure.

Over the years, though, 50,000 words has proven itself a good goal for a month's labors. Writing 50,000 words in a month breaks down to about 1,667 words per day. Most average typists will be able to dispatch that in an hour and a half, which makes it doable,

 ISN'T 50,000 WORDS MORE OF A NOVELLA?

While it's true that 50,000 words makes for a short novel, it does *not* make what you are about to write a novella.

Novellas, as decreed by the World Literary Council in its precedent-setting 1956 ruling, are "weak-willed, half-hearted novels" that "lack the gumption to make it to 50,000 words,"

which they very accurately describe as "the very precipice of novelhood."

But mainly the reason to avoid describing your upcoming work as a novella is because it doesn't impress people the way *novel* does. Remember: You're writing a novel next month. Don't let anyone tell you differently.

even for people with full-time jobs and chaotic home lives. Fifty thousand words is also just large enough for someone writing concisely to sketch an entire story arc within its borders.

And yet, despite its short stature, a 50,000-word novel is no cakewalk. Only about 17 percent of National Novel Writing Month participants reach the 50,000-word finish line every year, and some have argued that the number should be lowered.

I think the number is perfect. Because you're covering so much ground, so quickly, the high number forces you to lower your expectations for your prose, to write for quantity over quality, and to stop being so hard on yourself. And this, for a first draft, is the pathway to genius.

LOW EXPECTATIONS, HIGH YIELD

If your fiction is anything like mine, you have long since become accustomed to the concept of underachievement. Celebrating your writing inadequacies, though, will likely be a new and somewhat uncomfortable prospect. Give it a try when you write your novel next month. The most important mental preparation you can do for the noveling month ahead is to realize the following: There is no pressure on you to write a brilliant first draft. Because no one ever writes a brilliant first draft.

It's true. When your novel first peeks its head into the world, it will look pretty much like every newborn: pasty, hairless, and utterly confused. This is the case no matter how talented you are, or how long you take to coax the thing into existence. Novels are simply too long and complex to nail on the first go-round. Anyone who tells you differently is a superhuman literary cyborg, and should not be trusted.

I'm not making this up. Flip through books on writing by Stephen King or Anne Lamott, and they say the same thing (without, of course, the crucial insights on cyborgs). To quote the mild-mannered, word-mincing Ernest Hemingway: "The first draft of anything is shit."

It's not just shit, though. It's *wonderful* shit. A first draft is an anything-goes space for you to roll up your sleeves and make a terrific mess. It is a place where the writer's battle plan is redrawn daily; a place where recklessness and risk-taking is rewarded, where half-assed planning and tangential writing can yield unexpectedly amazing results. It is, in short, a place for people like you and me.

And when it comes to the topsy-turvy world of the rough draft, the law of the land is best summed up in two words: Exuberant imperfection.

Exuberant Imperfection Defined

The first law of exuberant imperfection is essentially this: The quickest, easiest way to produce something beautiful and lasting is to risk making something horribly crappy.

Like most things associated with writing a novel in a month, this may not make a lot of sense on the surface. But there's proven psychology behind it. Namely, the older we get, the more scared we are

EXTRACURRICULAR FORAYS INTO EXUBERANT IMPERFECTION

Lowering your unrealistically high standards for your writing can be achieved more easily if you practice it in other life domains as well. In the coming weeks, loosen your control over your life. Sing off-key in public. Tell jokes, even if you can't exactly remember the punchlines. Stop proofreading the emails you send to friends. Try your hand at something you've long thought you might like but fear you'll be bad at. You'll probably feel uncomfortable and exposed at first, but you'll also find that the world is a lot more fun when you approach it with an exuberant imperfection.

to try new things. Especially things that might make us look stupid in public. (Women with boyfriends or husbands can see this in action by suggesting they take salsa dancing classes together.)

The reason for this is that, as grown-ups, we come to place undue importance on this thing called "competence." From the work world, we've learned that the way to get ahead in life is to brandish proficiency and know-how at anything that moves— co-workers, bosses, customers, and so on. We do this for a very good reason: to keep from getting fired.

In the workplace, the emphasis on professionalism makes great sense. No one wants to have his or her cerebellum doctored by a dilettante brain surgeon. But the emphasis on mastery has certain unseen psychological ramifications on the rest of our lives. You'd think, for instance, that this workaday obsession with competence would make our weekends a refuge for floundering forays into uncharted territories.

But what do we do when we have free time? The tried-and-true activities we've already perfected. Like talking on the phone. Or walking up and down stairs. Or getting drunk. The times we do actually make a point of stepping out of our normal routine, we tend to get flustered when we don't get the hang of it right away. This is especially true with artistic endeavors. At the first awkward line of prose or botched brushstroke, we hurriedly pack away the art sup- plies and scamper back to our comfortable domains of proficiency. Better a quitter than a failure, our subconscious reasoning goes.

Exuberant imperfection allows you to circumvent those limiting feelings entirely. It dictates that the best way to tackle daunting, paralysis-inducing challenges is to give yourself permission to make mistakes, and then go ahead and make them.

In the context of novel writing, this means you should lower the bar from "best-seller" to "would not make someone vomit." Exuberant imperfection encourages you to write uncritically, to experiment, to break your time-honored rules of writing just to see what happens. In a first draft, nothing is permanent, and everything is fixable. So stay loose and flexible, and keep your expectations very, very low.

It sounds like a recipe for a disastrous novel, I know. But as you'll discover when you start writing, lowered expectations don't necessarily translate into lowered quality. Exuberant imperfection is not a surefire path to bad writing so much as it is a necessary mental reshuffling, a psychological sleight-of-hand that takes the pressure off and helps you tolerate the drivel that greases the wheels of genius. In your first draft, the ratio of muck to mastery may be somewhat disappointing. But that's just life as a draft-wranglin' novelist. It will all get better in time. For now, quantity—not quality—is of primary importance.

And embracing exuberant imperfection will do much more than just help keep your word counts soaring in the coming month. By giving yourself the gift of imperfection, you tap into the realms of intuition and imagination that your hypercritical brain normally censors. These are the left-of-center dialogue exchanges and strange character quirks that end up forming the most memorable and delightful parts of your novel.

This torrent of thoughts and ideas is exhilarating and scary, and absolutely, absolutely essential to getting a first draft written in such a short amount of time.

WRITING IN PACKS

Along with a rigid, rigorous deadline and an anything-goes writing approach, there is one more prerequisite for pulling a surprisingly competent book out of yourself quickly: finding company.

Ideally, you will find people interested in taking the noveling plunge alongside you, cranking out their own questionable masterworks in the same month you do. But "company" can also simply mean finding nonwriting friends and loved ones who agree to check in on your progress throughout the month, providing a little friendly support along the way.

If you've been writing fiction for a while, you may already be a member of a writing group. The typical writing group, however, is actually a reading group; it's there to give feedback on works each member produces in isolation. The group you want to form now is one where you meet up only to write. No sharing. No critiques. No feedback whatsoever. Just pure, unadulterated output.

For most people (and I used to count myself among them), writing is a private act, and the thought of writing *en masse* sounds both terrifying and highly unproductive. Give it a shot. You'd be surprised how much the clack of other people typing brings out the novelist beast in you, and how much the push of friendly competition will keep you working on your story even when you're ready to kill all of your characters.

The goal, ultimately, is to move your novel from the realm of private suffering to a matter of public record. The help of a writing community and the fear of public failure are both invaluable motivators, and both have a way of turning an already strong 50,000-word mission into a fait accompli.

ACTIVATING YOUR DEADLINE

Before you can let everyone know that you're writing a novel in a month, you first need to square it with yourself. So go get that calendar and pick out the best month for you to do this. No month is going to be perfect, but here are some signs of a good one: abysmal weather, a built-in three-day weekend, and a month where your family or housemates might accidentally be beamed to another galaxy for thirty days.

Barring that, all months are pretty much equal. The one bit of advice I do offer in choosing your timeframe is to write over the

WHAT DOES 50,000 WORDS LOOK LIKE?

The book you're holding in your hands is now almost exactly 50,000 words. Some other novels checking in at around 50,000 words in length include:

The Great Gatsby
by F. Scott Fitzgerald

Brave New World
by Aldous Huxley

The Blue Flower
by Penelope Fitzgerald

The Catcher in the Rye
by J. D. Salinger

The Hitchhiker's Guide to the Galaxy
by Douglas Adams

The Adventures of Tom Sawyer
by Mark Twain

True Grit
by Charles Portis

Generation X: Tales of an Accelerated Culture
by Douglas Coupland

Happy All the Time
by Laurie Colwin

Ghost Children
by Sue Townsend

Of Mice and Men
by John Steinbeck

However, keep in mind that the 50,000-word rough draft you write next month will likely balloon out by 10,000 to 50,000 words in a rewrite. The typical paperback you see on a bookstore shelf is about 100,000 words, with shorter genre fiction, like serial romances or sci-fi tie-ins, coming in at 50,000 to 70,000 words.

course of a calendar month, rather than simply picking thirty-one consecutive days. Structure and drama are both essential in the coming endeavor, and both will be heightened if your deadline coincides with a month's end.

Once you've picked your month, just read and sign the *No Plot? No Problem!* "Month-Long Novelist Agreement and Statement of Understanding (Deadline #A30/31/50k)" on the facing pages. Then meet me at chapter two. We have some planning to do.

THE MONTH-LONG NOVELIST AGREEMENT
AND STATEMENT OF UNDERSTANDING

I hereby pledge my intent to write a 50,000-word novel in one month's time. By invoking an absurd, month-long deadline on such an enormous undertaking, I understand that notions of "craft," "brilliance," and "competency" are to be chucked right out the window, where they will remain, ignored, until they are retrieved for the editing process. I understand that I am a talented person, capable of heroic acts of creativity, and I will give myself enough time over the course of the next month to allow my innate gifts to come to the surface, unmolested by self-doubt, self-criticism, and other acts of self-bullying.

During the month ahead, I realize I will produce clunky dialogue, clichéd characters, and deeply flawed plots. I agree that all of these things will be left in my rough draft, to be corrected and/or excised at a later point. I understand my right to withhold my manuscript from all readers until I deem it completed. I also acknowledge my right as author to substantially inflate both the quality of the rough draft and the rigors of the writing process should such inflation prove useful in garnering me respect and attention, or freedom from participation in onerous household chores.

I acknowledge that the month-long, 50,000-word deadline I set for myself is absolute and unchangeable, and that any failure to meet the deadline, or any effort on my part to move the deadline once the adventure has begun, will invite well-deserved mockery from friends and family. I also acknowledge that, upon successful completion of the stated noveling objective, I am entitled to a period of gleeful celebration and revelry, the duration and intensity of which may preclude me from participating fully in workplace activities for days, if not weeks, afterward.

Signed   **Date**

Novel Start Date   **Novel Deadline**

CHAPTER  2

Time-Finding, News-Breaking,
and a Step-by-Step Guide to
Transforming Loved Ones into Effective
Agents of Guilt and Terror

Tim Lohnes was in pain. The thirty-year-old Oakland cartographer was less than a week into NaNoWriMo, and his story was floundering.

"I just didn't know what to do with my characters," he says. "Plus, my wrists were hurting, and I had three work projects that were keeping me up until 2:00 A.M. every night."

Tim tried to resurrect the story in the second week, managing to get his word count up to 12,000. But it just wasn't happening, and that's when Tim stopped working on the book entirely.

Then, with three days left in the writing month, Tim got a new idea for his book. "I just started feeling it," he says.

Tim dove into his tale for a third time. And this time it caught. Tim raced against time, sleeping five hours a night, pounding out 38,000 words in three days, typing "The End" at the 50,006-word mark. There were fifteen minutes left to go on the month's clock.

All of this would be utterly extraordinary if Tim didn't do it this way every year. Yep. In five years of doing NaNoWriMo, Tim has always written most of his book, and become a winner every time, at the last minute. And he's not alone. In last year's NaNoWriMo, hundreds of writers leapt from four-digit word counts to the 50,000-word finish line in the final few days of the contest.

Tim—and the other writers who have learned to turn procrastination into performance art—would be the first to admit that writing an entire manuscript in three days exacts a high toll on your book and your body. But their rocket-fueled exploits underline an important fact of this whole endeavor: Writing 50,000 words of fiction really doesn't take *that* much time. Slow writers find they can write about 800 words of novel per hour; a speedy writer (and good typist) can easily do twice that. Which means that the whole novel, from start to finish, will take an average writer about 55 hours to write.

If you had the luxury of writing eight hours a day, seven days a week, you could begin on a Monday morning and be wrapping up your epilogue in time for brunch on Sunday.

The truth is, though, that few of us have the luxury of writing eight hours a day, seven days a week. In fact, between school, jobs, and the host of other daily events that fill our lives, carving 55 hours of quiet time, however small that number looks on paper, ends up being quite a challenge.

Enter the Time Finder.

FINDING YOUR FORGO-ABLE
WITH THE TIME FINDER

The Time Finder is to novel-planning what the Jaws of Life are to accident scenes. But rather than extracting precious things from tight places, the Time Finder does the opposite: It helps wedge large valuables into impossibly small spaces. The tool is the ideal way to discover the answer to the inevitable question, "Where the hell am I going to find the time to write a novel?"

To use it, you only need some paper, a pen, and some red, blue, and green highlighters (or colored pencils). You'll also need five minutes a night for seven nights in a row. And before you start complaining about getting homework already, let it be known: There are treats involved.

Here's how it works: Before you go to bed every night, sit down with your paper and pen, and write down everything you did that day, broken down into half-hour increments. Start with the moment you woke up and carry it through to the time you turned on the Time Finder. For me—a freelance writer—yesterday's list would look like this:

8:30–9:00 Made and consumed breakfast.

9:00–9:30 Showered, brushed teeth, got dressed. Laid back down in bed. Reluctantly got back up again.

9:30–10:30 Emailed friends.

10:30–1:30 Worked.

1:30–2:30 Ate lunch while emailing friends and surfing the Internet.

2:30–5:00 Worked some more.

5:00–5:30 Drove to the post office. Returned.

5:30–6:00 Read the *Onion* and watched dumb music videos online.

6:00–6:30 Checked email.

6:30–7:00 Talked on the phone, considered cleaning the apartment.
7:00–7:30 Went for short walk.
7:30–8:30 Went out to dinner with girlfriend (note to self: never again eat a deep-fried anything that's referred to as an "awesome blossom").
8:30–9:00 Took a stab at actually cleaning up apartment, halfheartedly washed some dishes, called parents.
9:00–9:30 Hastily assembled package I was supposed to send for Mom's birthday two weeks ago.
9:30–10:00 Paid bills.
10:00–11:00 Worked.
11:00–12:00 Skimmed the newspaper, read a little bit of a novel.
12:00–12:30 Remembered I was supposed to email an editor about an assignment. Wrote email and sent it off.
12:30 Activated Time Finder.

After you've finished each daily log, reward yourself with a delicious, nonnutritious treat, and then go to sleep. (Sleep, by the way, should not be included on the Time Finder's list of items, as hoarding as much sleep as possible every night is the birthright of amateur writers everywhere.)

After you've carefully documented your activities for one week, bust out the highlighters or colored pencils, and go to town. First, go through and circle or underline every REQUIRED activity in red. These are the top-tier items that you have to do every day or risk unemployment, eviction, expulsion, or mental collapse. Things in this category would be basic acts of personal hygiene, commutes to work or school, actual working, running work-related errands, eating meals, shuttling friends or family around, grocery shopping, and paying bills.

Next, go through the lists and mark the HIGHLY DESIRED activities in blue. In this category go the things that, if push came to shove, you could get by without doing for a month, but which would cause major stress or hardship. This second tier of activities could include exercising, returning social phone calls and emails, attending friends' birthday parties, or going to professional or religious get-togethers.

Finally, take that last color and mark all the FORGO-ABLE activities that you could give up for a month without courting disaster. This includes Internet surfing and chat-room trawling, online shopping, TV-watching, making art, nonessential home repairs, hobby-based tinkering, and recreational reading.

Okay, now it's time to shift the Time Finder into overdrive. Go through the forgo-able items, and add up how many hours you spend per day, on average, in their pursuit. As you can see from my list, I tend to spend about three hours every day doing things that I could sacrifice for thirty days without my life falling apart.

If, like me, you've found that you're spending between an hour and a half to two hours a day on forgo-able items, you're golden. These will be your sacrificial lambs next month. Say good-bye to them now, and know they will still be there when you pick them up again in thirty days.

NOVELING THROUGH THE SPACE-TIME CONTINUUM: THE NANOWRIMO TEMPORAL VORTEX

In my forays into month-long noveling, I've repeatedly noticed something that seems, on the surface, impossible. Which is this: When I introduce novel writing into my schedule, I actually seem to have *more* time, for running errands and goofing off. Other NaNoWriMo participants have confirmed the phenomenon, which seems to stem from a short-term willingness to maximize every minute of the day to startlingly productive effect. A side effect of this is that the moments that you do choose to spend in leisure activities become imbued with a sort of technicolor radiance—with everyday pleasures like unhurried conversations and ambling window-shopping taking on a near-sexual lushness. Strange, but true.

When I'm writing a novel, I stop Internet surfing entirely, limit my leisure reading, and spend much less weeknight time with (non-noveling) friends. Other writers use the opportunity to pare back conversations with their in-laws and stop doing yard work. The choice is yours; all you need to do is find an hour and a half or so per day in the forgo-able category and you've got a green light to write.

If you can't trim the fat you need from the forgo-able items, you'll need to slice into the meat of your highly desired activities. Because these are more important, the best approach is to cut down on frequency rather than eliminate them entirely. Plan on skipping a few meetings, ducking out of birthday parties early, or making your child hitchhike home from school a couple of days a week.

If you find yourself dipping into the "required" category to come up with the hours, congratulations. You are in the top .5 percent of busy people everywhere. The good news about this is that you've only survived this long by multitasking at an Olympic level. You'll be able to bring all those keen time-management skills to bear on your novel. If you haven't had a heart attack yet, odds are good you probably won't next month either.

Let's assume, though, that you, like most people, can get ten to fourteen hours a week through some basic leisure-time restrictions. If that's the case, leave everything else in your life alone. It may be tempting to use the novel as a cornerstone for a total lifestyle over-haul, but this is a decidedly bad time to implement ambitious changes in your life.

In fact, the best thing you can do for yourself, your manuscript, and those around you is to keep as many of your old routines as possible. Being available for a minimum of social activities helps keep your mind fresh for the book, and also forestalls mutiny among your friends and family.

THE GOLDEN RULE OF SCHEDULING

Though every productive noveling schedule is unique, and what works for one frantic writer won't necessarily work for another, there *is* one golden rule you should keep in mind when laying out your writing schedule: Don't take more than two nights off from your novel in a row.

Taking three or more nights away from your book back to back to back will not only stall whatever momentum you've developed in the story, it will also give your brain too much time to come up with doubts and other foot-dragging assessments of your work. In the same way cults tend to keep recent converts inside the compound walls, so should you make sure your brain doesn't go AWOL for too long from your book.

SCHEDULING YOUR WRITING TIME

Which brings us to the important question: How to allocate the soon-to-be-liberated hours the Time Finder just uncovered? Pacing is obviously important, but what is a good pace? Should you write every day? Every other day? On weekdays only? Does the onset of a bad mood mean you get to skip a planned writing session? What about an exploding pancreas?

Unfortunately, there are no hard-and-fast answers to any of these questions (save the case of exploding body parts, which warrants a one-day writing exemption). Even professional novelists have wildly conflicting theories about the ideal times and durations for writing sessions.

The chief tactic in formulating a winning battle plan for your noveling schedule is to try a variety of approaches early on, discover what works best for you, and use it relentlessly thereafter.

My personal technique is to write for two hours per night, three or four weeknights per week. I follow that up on weekends with three, two-hour sessions on either Saturday or Sunday.

Why do I do this? Habit. And because it seems to work. It also gives me one or two weeknights and one entire weekend day to relax and hang out with friends. This makes it exponentially less likely that I'll kill myself or those around me, and I still tend to arrive at the 50,000-word point a couple of days before the month ends.

Some NaNoWriMo participants do all of their writing in the morning before work, taking advantage of the relative quiet and the pleasant caffeine rush of the predawn hours. Still others make a point of nabbing half of the day's word-count quota on their lunch break and typing out the rest on their train ride home.

We'll get into the pros and cons of various noveling locations in chapter three. For now, the best way to approach your scheduling is with a light heart and an open mind. Because inevitably over the course of the month, you'll encounter a variety of emergencies at work and home that will curtail your chapters and muffle your muse. Friends will pick your noveling month to have relationship meltdowns. Your three favorite bands will come to town on the one night you'd set aside to finally get caught up on your word count. And your computer, which has worked flawlessly for the past five years, will explode in an apocalyptic series of error screens and electronic moans.

When this happens, just go with it. Sometimes taking a night off to go to that concert is the best thing you can do for your novel. And other times, you'll need to ask your friends to nail two-by-fours across your study door to make sure you have no way of fleeing your writing responsibilities. Having a ready supply of concert tickets *and* three-inch nails on hand, depending on your progress and mood, is the surest path to scheduling success.

Hope for the Best, Plan for the Worst

Even with all the vagaries of the novel-writing process, there *are* a few problems you can anticipate. Week One, for instance, is much easier than Week Two. It's a good idea to set aside a little extra time in the first seven days to rack up as many words as possible before the going gets tough.

Other predictable problems vary depending on personality. I, for one, am an inveterate procrastinator. While I regale my friends every year with the same wild-eyed promises about getting *way* ahead of my word-count quota early and staying far out in front of the writing pack the whole month, in truth I'm always struggling a little toward the end to finish the book on time.

Because of my steadfast, rock-solid procrastinating ways, I've learned to keep the entire final week and weekend of the month free of social obligations, no matter how enticing the parties or dinners or concerts sound. I make sure any trips I need to take happen in the beginning or middle of the month. I also do my best to reduce my workload (or, ahem, fall deathly ill) on the final Thursday and Friday of the event. Usually, I don't need all the time I set aside for myself, but the few times when eye strain or wrist problems have slowed my typing toward the end of the month, having those extra hours available has been priceless.

Yes, there *is* something a little defeatist about accepting one's slacking ways rather than trying to fix them. That's a worry, though, for another month. The healthiest, most productive approach to writing is to acknowledge your weak spots early on, and build a writing plan that plays to your strengths and works around your liabilities.

Once you have your plan in place, you're ready to move on to the next important step: finding a support network for encouragement and companionship on your upcoming voyage.

RALLYING THE TROOPS

For Trena Taylor, the decision to write a novel in a month didn't net her quite the outpourings of support she'd hoped.

"The announcement was greeted by a steady stream of blinking," the thirty-four-year-old Londoner and two-time NaNoWriMo winner says. "Total incomprehension. Most people just couldn't get 'round the idea that someone might actually *want* to write a novel, never mind the timeframe. Why spend a month writing a book when it only takes five minutes to buy one from the shops, was the general attitude."

Ah, friends and family. The compassionate souls who will be your cheerleaders and voices of reason; the ones who will pick you up off the floor and set you gently back at the computer keyboard. And also the ones who are most likely to poke merciless fun at this ambitious, artistic plan you've dragged home.

Whether those closest to you love or hate the idea of you spending a month slaving over a novel, it's essential that they know about your plans. In the same way you wouldn't think about going on a long trip without checking in with your loved ones, you should make sure you brief everyone about your literary agenda.

Why? Because for all their potential helpfulness, your intimates can also make your thirty days in novel-land very, very difficult. They can take your newfound shut-in tendencies personally, erode your willpower through succulent diversions, or demand extra amounts of your time just when you need it most for the book.

Mostly, though, you should talk to them because they are probably harboring secret noveling urges as well. And nothing diminishes the pain of extraordinary labors like having a friendly someone toiling there alongside you.

The Joys of Writing Partners

Novel writing is the perfect social activity. Granted, it is a social activity where no one is allowed to talk. And one where much of the pre- and postevent socializing consists of tearful laments about the deplorable state of one's writing and the meagerness of one's talents.

Maybe I have a strange idea of social activities, but this to me is heaven.

And a productive heaven at that. Writing with a partner (or three or four) helps all parties tap into the pool of competitive energy that forms when several people are working toward the same goal. When noveling with someone else, you have a pacer, a motivator, and a sympathetic ear for sharing the triumphs and tragedies of your novel. It's more productive and *a lot* more fun.

From your immediate family to long-forgotten classmates, chances are good that *someone* you know will take you up on the offer. And if no one in your immediate area is up for the challenge, pitch the idea to friends and relatives in faraway towns. You may not be able to novel in coffeeshops together, but you can have nightly check-ins via phone or email.

Filling the Home Team Bleachers

Just because someone declines the opportunity to come along on the writing journey doesn't mean that he or she can't be an essential part of the trip.

RISKY BUSINESS: COMING CLEAN TO CO-WORKERS ABOUT YOUR NOVEL

Some month-long novelists have found some of their most vocal supporters among co-workers. But unless you work for an incredibly understanding company or have very close friends at work, I'd recommend not mentioning your project to fellow employees. Superman was Clark Kent to his co-workers, and you might want to be similarly discreet about your new superhero novel-writing powers around officemates. Not because they won't be encouraging, but because word about your efforts will inevitably make it back to your boss, who will then know exactly who to come to when someone prints multiple copies of a two-hundred-page document on the office laser printer at the end of the month.

DOING THE NUMBERS: WHERE YOU SHOULD BE ON EACH DAY OF THE WORD PARADE

We'll do the worst-case scenario math, and assume you're writing your novel in a thirty-day month.

Day 1: 1,667 words
Day 2: 3,334 words
Day 3: 5,001 words
Day 4: 6,668 words
Day 5: 8,335 words
Day 6: 10,002 words
Day 7: 11,669 words
Day 8: 13,336 words
Day 9: 15,003 words
Day 10: 16,670 words
Day 11: 18,337 words
Day 12: 20,004 words
Day 13: 21,671 words
Day 14: 23,338 words
Day 15: 25,005 words
Day 16: 26,672 words
Day 17: 28,339 words
Day 18: 30,006 words
Day 19: 31,673 words
Day 20: 33,340 words
Day 21: 35,007 words
Day 22: 36,674 words
Day 23: 38,341 words
Day 24: 40,008 words
Day 25: 41,675 words
Day 26: 43,342 words
Day 27: 45,009 words
Day 28: 46,676 words
Day 29: 48,343 words
Day 30: 50,000 words

From cooking you the occasional dinner to checking in on your progress and mental stability, your support network of nonwriting friends will be invaluable in helping you survive the noveling slog. Because these are also the people most likely to be affected by your writing-inspired mood swings, your possible shortages of free time, and your substantially diminished regard for cleanliness ("I'll shower tomorrow, honey, I *promise!*"), it's a good idea to make sure they are on board.

When making my pitch for support to my loved ones every year, I always touch on the following four talking points:

Amateur writers who take years and years to write their rough drafts are sentencing themselves and those around them to a constant barrage of "novel guilt." This is the hand-wringing, esteem-squishing sense of constant self disappointment that accompanies any project that doesn't get worked on as often it should. By writing your entire rough draft in a month, you are not so much taking yourself out of your loved ones' lives for weeks as you are *giving* yourself to them for the years and years to come. By compressing all the procrastination and ensuing self-loathing into thirty manageable days, you'll be more pleasant to be around the rest of the time. (Don't mention the word "rewrite" until much, much later.)

With all the pressure of cranking out a book-length work of fiction in such a desperately short amount of time, you will be in need of fun, reviving distractions at various points throughout the month. And you'll have more time for socializing than you, or they, think. By removing the forgo-able items from your schedule, you'll likely have a few goofing-off hours per week that didn't exist before. You'll be busy, yes, but not *that* busy.

Those closest to us are also the ones who have heard all of our earnestly proclaimed, unfulfilled New Year's resolutions about gym-going, healthier eating, and other unrealistic pursuits. Your best friends are also the most likely to see this novel-in-a-month plan as another of your charmingly crackpot self-improvement schemes. Don't be offended if you encounter some good-natured ribbing; the idea of writing a novel in a month deserves to be laughed at. When the chuckles die down, though, do your best to make it clear that, however ridiculous the whole escapade may sound, you plan on seeing it through to completion. Also make it clear that, when you are a best-selling author, you will use a portion of your vast fortune to reward your supporters and destroy those who scoffed at you.

TALKING POINT 4: I need your help.

Everyone loves helping an underdog triumph against insurmountable odds. Talk to your best friends about all the obligations and chores you'll be juggling while you write, and have them brainstorm possible solutions and time-savers. You'll likely find a plethora of volunteers ready to help you get the small things accomplished so you'll have more time to go toe-to-toe with that literary Goliath.

TURNING CLOSE FRIENDS INTO OBLIGATIONS

Gentle encouragement from your friends and family, however, is just the start. Warm smiles and you-can-do-it emails won't help you keep your butt in the chair when you're ready to give up in the middle of Week Two. After collecting a group of cheerleaders, the next step is to leverage all their goodwill into usable quantities of *fear*.

Yep. Terror is the amateur novelist's best friend. Without some amount of it pushing you onward toward your goal, you're going to lose momentum and quit. There are just too many other, more sensible things to do with your time than try to write a novel in a month, and all of these more interesting alternatives will become irresistible if you don't have some fear binding you to your word-processing device.

Happily, with a little work, your friends and family can terrify you in ways you'd never imagined.

HOW TO HOST RUTHLESSLY PRODUCTIVE GROUP-WRITING EVENTS

If you don't have a laptop that allows you to take your writing out into public, bring the public home to you. Hosting a writing day (or, casting your net more widely, a "creative day") in your home or apartment will ensure you stay on track, and will make the chore of writing more fun. If you do invite friends over, make it clear in your invitation that this will be a *work* session, and that attendees who don't maintain a minimum level of productivity will be beaten. Include a clear start time and end time in your invitation, and encourage people to be punctual.

Make sure you have enough tables, desks, and chairs set up to accommodate everyone's particular work needs, and make sure that a clock is clearly visible to everyone. Brew up a pot of coffee or tea, and have lots of noncrumbly, nonoily treats on hand so people can snack without worrying about their keyboards.

After everyone's had a chance to settle in, announce a schedule. Thirty or forty minutes of work followed by a ten-minute break is a good one. But it's up to you. Whether you allow talking during the work sessions is also your call, but if you okay conversation during the work period, be sure to have headphones or earplugs on hand so you don't get distracted. Ask all attendees to turn off the ringers on their cell phones, and set a timer so everyone knows exactly when each session ends and the glorious break time begins.

Should anyone continue to type after the alarm marking the end of the session sounds, chop off their fingers. Don't be afraid to be a tyrant.

Bragging as a Tool for Self-Motivation

When inculcating a healthy amount of fear, bragging is an indispensable tool. Nothing makes it more difficult to back down from a task than having boasted about it, in great detail, to all of your friends and loved ones. Think about it: Do you really want to be the butt of jokes *every* time novels are mentioned? For the *rest of your life?* Or have to hear your mother sigh when she learns that you have botched yet another attempt at making something of yourself?

I don't either. Which is why I make a point of laying a solid foundation of bragging *way* before I've thought about plot or setting or character. My ultimate goal is to back myself so far into a corner before the month even starts that I have no choice but to stay on course with the word count, no matter how dismally off-track my novel gets in the weeks that follow.

In this way, bragging is an essential device for creating expectations. Not for genius prose, mind you. No, what you want to do is set up expectations for *completion*. For staying on track. For seeing it through to 50,000 words.

Some people pay personal trainers thousands of dollars to receive this sort of ongoing, disappointment-based motivation. Smart people get it from friends and family for free. Begin talking about your imminent ascent of the noveling ladder immediately after you have those first discussions with your friends about the thirty-day plunge.

In our wired age, email is the most efficient path to acquiring mass motivation. Send out boasting emails to everyone you know about your quest. Look up long-lost classmates to inform them you will be a novelist in a couple of months. If you have a novel-friendly office, spam your department with your good writing news. This kind of outreach nets you, the writer, two invaluable things:

1) Constant motivational/envious/resentful check-ins from friends throughout the month about how the novel is going.

2) An irresistible invitation to widespread mockery should you not actually reach 50,000 words.

Betting the Bank

Lustily bragging about your upcoming noveling exploits often segues beautifully into the next recommended prewriting strategy: leveling huge, possibly crippling debts against the outcome of your novel.

For Andrew Johnson, twenty-nine, of Christchurch, New Zealand, the opportunity came at the office.

"A disbelieving workmate challenged me when I said, 'I bet I can do it,'" recalls the three-time NaNoWriMo winner.

"'Okay,' I said. 'How much?' I took fifty-dollar bets from *any* person willing to stake their cash on me being unable to complete the novel."

Andrew finished out the month with both a new novel and a little extra pocket money. Unfortunately, he had to retire the scheme soon thereafter.

"Oddly, it only worked for one year," Andrew writes. "Those who get stung by a fanatical NaNoWriMo writer once are going to avoid being stung again in the future."

If you're having trouble finding people kind enough to bet against you, you can still leverage the same motivating fear of total financial ruin through "conditional donations."

This path was pioneered by a month-long novelist writing outside of NaNoWriMo. In May 2001, an aspiring writer named Paul Griffiths announced that if he failed in his quest to write a 60,000-word novel in one month, he would donate his entire life savings to the National Rifle Association.

Paul was not a fan of the NRA, and was very enamored of his savings account, and these two things combined to give him all the incentive he needed to get the novel finished.

To follow in Paul's footsteps, here's all you have to do:

1) Find an organization you detest. If you are stuck for ideas, call your favorite charity and ask for a list of groups who are out to destroy them. Be sure not to choose a good or righteous cause, as this may make giving up on your novel mid-month feel like a philanthropic act.

2) Once you've selected a suitably villainous group, break out your checkbook and write a check to them. Make the amount large enough to wreak havoc on your finances, but small enough that you won't be tempted to put a stop payment on the check should it ever actually make it to them.

3) Seal the check in an envelope, address it, and then give the envelope to a friend with strict instructions to return the money to you should you complete 50,000 words of fiction in a month's time. Should you fail to reach 50,000 words, he or she should do you the favor of dropping the envelope in the mail.

4) Inform your friend that someone posing as you may return in thirty days to plead for the money, claiming the whole novel-writing thing was a dumb idea. If this happens, make your friend promise to restrain the imposter until the police arrive.

And there you have it: intense literary motivation for the price of a stamp. And when you actually do finish the novel in thirty days, you are both a novelist and a righteous crusader, having kept a small fortune out of the hands of evildoers. Way to go, superhero!

Chore-Based Betting

Many of us, however, go through our lives unencumbered with such fiscal distractions as savings accounts, retirement funds, or petty cash, and therefore have nothing to potentially squander on diabolical organizations.

No matter how poor we may be, though, there is one thing we can always wager: our bodies. Those with no savings to put on the line should sit down with friends and set up a series of chore-based ultimatums. Should you only write 30,000 words next month, for instance, you agree to scrub a friend's kitchen floor. A 20,000-word total means mowing lawns for a month. And should you fail to break 10,000 words, you agree to scoop the poop of your friend's fiercely incontinent dog for an entire year.

You'll find that friends and family warm to this plan immediately. For guaranteed novel-writing results, it's best to construct a web of miserable chore-based bets that would essentially occupy your weekends until you die.

For thirty-five-year-old, five-time NaNoWriMo winner Dan Strachota of San Francisco, the conditional betting took place on the home front. "The second year I did NaNoWriMo, my girlfriend and I wrote together at adjacent computers," Dan remembers. "In order to motivate ourselves we would make wagers over who could write the most words in thirty minutes. It would get pretty competitive, as the punishments for losing grew more and more heinous—from easy stuff like having to give backrubs and sing a capella songs to harder things like running up the street half naked, doing funny dances, and kissing random strangers."

Ah, the timeless power of tender, loving humiliation. Follow Dan's example and get creative in your shackling of yourself to your writing instrument. And remember: A little fear goes a long, long way.

CHAPTER  3

Noveling Nests,

   Magical Tools,

and a Growing Stockpile of

   Delicious Incentives

In her search for a quiet place to write, Karla Akins quickly found that locking herself away in her study brought no relief from the tempests brewing in the house.

"A closed door with children in the house is nothing more than an invitation to bang, kick, scream, and cry," advises Akins, a 42-year-old one-time NaNoWriMo winner from North Manchester, Indiana. "The teenager will be in an emotional crisis with his girl-friend, and the younger ones are sure you simply cannot survive without being in their presence."

Karla's quest for some writing solace did turn up one unique environment where the children were much less likely to intrude.

"I do a lot of brainstorming and 'writing' on the toilet," she says. "I keep a notebook or small tape recorder with me all the time. It's amazing what kinds of things will come to me while having my 'quiet time.'"

Writers with children can relate to Karla's nomadic quest for quiet. But even if the only other living things you share your home with are house plants and dust mites, finding a perfect place to write is not easy.

In this chapter, we'll look at the pros and cons of potential noveling environments, from coffeeshops to cars to cheap motels. And after we look at where you might write, we'll go shopping for the tools—edible and otherwise—that you'll need to gather for the mammoth literary task ahead.

WRITING AT HOME

Home is the best option most of us have for pounding out novels. It's familiar, it's open twenty-four hours a day, it's relatively private, and the food and drinks on the menu are as cheap as you'll find anywhere outside of a soup kitchen.

The advantages of home-based working, though, are also its shortcomings. Because your house, apartment, or dorm room is so familiar, you'll likely find it difficult to draw a firm line between "novel time" and "puttering time," "family time," or, most harrowingly, "dishwashing time." A quick trip to the fridge for some glucose reinforcements can turn into an hour-long rearranging of the canned goods in your cupboards. Phones ring. Email lurks. And because you can work as late as you want without employees trying to shoo you out, you're bound to be less focused in your writing, letting noveling take a backseat to other pressing chores that arise.

All these liabilities can be minimized with a few tips:

1) Isolate yourself as much as possible.

If you live with other people, try to find a spot where you won't be disturbed. Be creative about it. Try writing in closets, bathrooms, or garages. Anywhere with a door that closes is your friend. If you don't have access to a room with a door, arrange your computer so you're facing a wall, and get some oversized headphones or earplugs. Also, if you can do so without causing an uproar among your family or housemates, disconnect the phone and Web connections. You can return any calls or emails after the session is over.

2) Create uninterrupted blocks of time, and limit yourself to them.

Make it clear to yourself and anyone you live with that you will be working, uninterrupted, for a set amount of time—at which point you will stop and rejoin the normal, non-noveling human race. Knowing that you'll be working for a bounded amount of time helps keep you on task, and it will spare any housemates or family members from feeling like they need to tip-toe around you the whole night.

3) Make yourself comfortable.

Find a stable desk or table, and make sure your chair feels good and raises you up to a wrist-friendly typing level.

4) Don't write within view of a bed.

The sweet, sweet temptation of napping is simply too great. If you live in a studio apartment, or are otherwise obligated to write in your bedroom, do what I do: Pile a cumbersome assortment of boxes and other heavy items onto your bed to retard the onset of accidental slumbers.

5) Keep your writing area neat.

If you're anything like me, your life is chaotic enough already; give yourself the gift of sitting down to a tidy writing area each day. This doesn't mean, incidentally, that you can't storm and throw things around as you work. I find flinging balls of paper, pens, and other assorted office supplies across the room helps the whole writing process feel more romantically agonized, and I'll throw things for fun even when my novel is going well. But at the close of each session, just spend a couple of minutes picking up the papers, coffee mugs, wads of chewing tobacco, and half-eaten animal carcasses and move them all into the kitchen (where they can be more effectively ignored). That way, no matter how messy the rest of your living quarters get, your runway for the next day's literary adventure will be cleared for takeoff.

HOW DO I GET RID OF MY CHILDREN?

For parents, balancing the need for alone time with your kids' needs for, well, everything can add a difficult twist to an already challenging month. Here are tips from six parents who have learned how to be creative writer types and benevolent guardians at the same time.

"I decided it was time for the twins to start learning to prepare simple meals. I juggled my schedule so I could write when they weren't home or were asleep. Much of my writing was done between 4:30 and 6:30 A.M., then again at night. Be prepared to sacrifice sleep, but that's okay, because when you do finally sleep, your dreams are almost guaranteed to provoke interesting chains of thought."
—Amy Eason, 35, one-time NaNoWriMo winner from McDonough, Georgia; Amy lives with an eleven-year-old, thirteen-year-old twins, a fifteen-year-old, and a seventeen-year-old.

"With a small kid in the house, you have to steal time. Extra-long nap? Okay! Watch one more episode of the *Wiggles*? Sure! Of course, there is a backlash to that, but I figure December is the price to pay for the sins of November."
—Tom Ferland, 39, three-time NaNoWriMo winner from Redlands, California; Tom lives with a three-year-old.

"My daughter was eleven the first year I wrote a novel, so I did a lot of my writing in the cafe at the local bookstore and just turned her loose to amuse herself with books. She was very sad when November was over and we weren't spending hours upon hours at Borders."
—Rise Sheridan-Peters, 42, three-time NaNoWriMo winner from Washington, D.C.; Rise lives with a thirteen-year-old.

"I got a wireless keyboard, and we moved furniture so that I had the couch in front of my computer instead of a chair. She cuddled with me and I typed with her. And tried to keep her from adding to my word count. The 'me time' came into play in that my generous husband agreed that during the month of November,if he wanted a clean toilet, he could do it his damn self. I was in charge of the baby and the novel. He took care of everything else."
—Alexandra Queen, 28, three-time NaNoWriMo winner from Ripon, California; Alexandra lives with a two-year-old.

"The only advice I have for anyone who writes with a little kid in the house is to do it when they're not around. I suggest enlisting the help of a spouse/babysitter for the month, or planning to forgo sleep when the child is in bed. And TV. Lots of TV."
—Laurie Jackson, 39, two-time NaNoWriMo winner from Colorado Springs, Colorado; Laurie lives with a six-year-old.

"Making the commitment to write a novel is probably the biggest obstacle. Then, making it a priority is the other. If I didn't make it a priority for that day, it didn't get done. And with children, it truly won't get done if you aren't a little selfish and take that time out of the day to write. My advice to other moms is that if you have a story, then tell it. I always believe it's not just about us. It's about the fact that someone in the world needs to hear what we have to say, and we are letting them down if we don't write it."
—Karla Akins, 42, one-time NaNoWriMo winner from North Manchester, Indiana; Karla lives with eight-year-old twins, a thirteen-year-old, and an eighteen-year-old.

CREATING A NOVELING HEADQUARTERS
AWAY FROM HOME

For those not chained to desktop computers, the world is a particularly succulent noveling oyster. Laptops, PDAs, and pens and paper allow writers to take advantage of a host of wonderful, creativity-spiking writing milieus.

For me, I have to get out of the house to write. Though I live alone, I find the peace and quiet at home insufferably distracting and the siren song of my bed irresistible. I also find that my apartment, with its off-the-beaten-path location and cumbersome series of locks, has a real dearth of interesting-looking strangers wandering in off the street looking for coffee.

Working in public gives you that and more. Obsessive email checking is curtailed, the mood is more lively, and buckets of caffeine are sitting there for the asking. Because I have the attention span of an aphid, I tend to seek out new writing environments pretty frequently, particularly ones that are open late. In my search for noveling novelty, I've driven out to the airport to spend the day writing in the concourses, had day-long writing sessions in the local IKEA cafeteria (fantastic views over the San Francisco Bay!), and worked out more than one chapter in the swank, anonymous recesses of downtown hotel bars.

Of all the environments for writing outside the home, though, I've found none more amenable than the cafe.

Your Novel
(Coming Soon to a Coffeeshop Near You)

The allure of a coffeeshop for noveling is obvious: instant access to caffeine, comfortable seats, sturdy tables, and a nonstop stream of potential novel fodder walking by.

With wireless modems and powerful laptops so ubiquitous these days, the click of computer keys has become as common a coffeehouse noise as the whir of the milk steamer. The tech-friendly vibe of most cafes is great news for novel writers, and as you scope out cafes in your area keep an eye out for the following boons:

Plenty of outlets!

If your laptop is as old as mine, the key strategy is jockeying for a good position near the cafe's electrical outlets. A laptop uses a miniscule amount of power (about a cent per hour)—a cost you can karma-cly offset by supersizing your drink or getting something to nibble on while you write.

If you feel comfortable doing it, a good way to get around an otherwise great spot's shortage of outlets is to bring a powerstrip (or three-outlet extender) and an extension cord. I always keep both in my car in November for NaNoWriMo group writing sessions in coffeeshops (I also have a roll of electrical tape on hand in case the cord becomes a tripping hazard for other patrons).

Students!

Where there are students, there is inevitably a greater-than-average tolerance for "camping," the term staff use to describe people who set up shop at tables for hours at a time. Since your average writing session will probably be about two hours, you'd do well to find a place that won't start giving you the hairy eyeball if you nurse that latte for a while.

Quiet background music!

There's a coffeeshop near my house in Oakland that has it all: convenient location, strong java, comfy seats, and electrical outlets up the wazoo. The cafe, though, is always on the verge of going out of business. Why? Because the manager has a soft spot for lite rock at block-shaking volumes. Hall and Oates are painful at a murmur; turned up loud, they become a health hazard. Don't waste your time trying to write in a place where you can't concentrate.

As soulless as they can sometimes be, Starbucks coffeeshops are built for abuse by novelists; the music is usually surprisingly good (and inoffensively low) and all of them make a point of making outlets accessible to laptop users. And best of all, as long as you're not setting anything on fire, the staff doesn't care how long you stay.

Libraries

Like coffeeshops, libraries are starting to become more hip to the needs of laptop users, adding both electrical outlets and ethernet cables to the traditional study carrels. Unlike cafes, libraries will let you stay as long as you like without buying anything. You also have the instant advantage/distraction of being able to do research as you write.

The library's main drawback is usually an early closing time. If you live close to a university, though, chances are good there will be some college libraries that stay open until 11:00 P.M. or midnight. Call ahead to see if you need a student ID for entry.

Work

As two-time NaNoWriMo winner Irfon Ahmad can tell you, not all press is good press. When the thirty-two-year-old Torontonian was quoted in a newspaper article about the city's NaNoWriMo participants, his quiet literary project suddenly became a matter of public record at his office. With some surprising results.

"From that point onward," Irfon says, "everybody at my company would ask me about my word count and how the novel was going every day. I could pretty much work on it openly as long as nothing with a really tight deadline was looming. I think that my

DEDUCTING YOUR NOVELIST SHOPPING SPREE FROM YOUR TAXES

Want to save a bundle on your noveling notebook, pens, and reference novels? What about a discount on movie tickets and DVDs? A percentage off your rent or mortgage? Well, read on: As a novelist, you're entitled to deduct all of your novel-writing expenses from your taxes. Maybe.

I talked to Peter Abel, a CPA in Oakland, and asked him to explain the somewhat confusing criteria the IRS use when deciding what expenses amateur novelists can write off in the pursuit of their muse.

"If you're an artist," Peter says, "there is a great latitude in the things that you do in order to research your craft. The big issue is whether this is a hobby or whether this is a business."

If, like many of us, you are writing your novel just for the fun of it, you are out of luck. But if you do intend to someday make money from your writing, get thee to a CPA right away. Everything that furthers your novel-writing efforts ("research" trips to Majorca, cable TV, a new computer with a wall-sized plasma screen, etc.) can be deducted from your taxes, as long as you can prove you spent the money in an effort to produce a cash-generating manuscript.

According to Peter, the simplest way to prove your honorable mercantile intentions is to actually sell a book. Since the business of novel writing often consists of years of unprofitable struggle, the IRS allows you to also deduct expenses so long as you document *attempts* at profitability. These include postal receipts from sending out manuscripts, copies of query letters you send to editors or agents, and logs of phone calls you made hounding your local publisher. Oh, and keep a written record of all your efforts, and pay for everything you can by credit card or check so you'll have a proof of payment and a receipt. And know that claiming a deduction, especially deducting a home office, does increase your chances of being audited by a percentage point or two.

boss would have been willing to excuse me from meetings to write if I'd have asked. He was very excited about the whole thing."

While this sounds like a dream set-up for most of us, Irfon soon discovered the complicated nature of bringing personal projects into a working environment.

"It ended up acting as a huge deterrent from writing," Irfon laments. "Because everybody assumed that I would slip company time to write, I went out of my way to prove that I was being productive, and I didn't write at all during working hours. The year before, when I was being furtive about the whole thing, I probably wrote nearly a quarter of my novel at work."

That, in a nutshell, describes the office: It's a wonderful, horrible place to get work done. Its appeal as a novel workshop lies in the lengthy attendance it requires of us each week, and chances are good that while using the Time Finder in chapter two you drooled over all the red-underlined hours you spend at work every day. If you spent just a fraction of your workday typing on your novel, you'd be able to get the whole book written on company time.

Yet, as Irfon's story indicates, work can be a surprisingly difficult place to get things done. The most ethically unencumbered route is to come in to work early or stay late. This also gives you the advantage of writing with fewer distracting co-workers around coming up to ask how your novel is going.

Fellow Toronto resident Michele Marques, a thirty-nine-year-old one-time NaNoWriMo winner—who used a Palm PDA with a collapsible keyboard—found her company's breakroom to be a fantastic place to write.

"I think the workplace cafeteria is greatly underrated," Michele reports. "There's good lighting, a flat surface, and a lunch hour. If you bring your lunch, you only have reheat and you're ready to write."

And then there's the matter of actually noveling during working hours. The moral question of stealing company time to work on your novel is a toughie. If you do decide to novel during working hours, there are four practical pointers to keep in mind to make the writing as productive as possible.

1) Tell few (if any) co-workers you're writing the novel until you're finished with it.

As Irfon's story proves, once word gets out about your literary feat-in-progress, everyone will start thinking you're working on your novel even when you're doing actual work.

NO PLOT? NO PROBLEM!

2) Know that, unless you are working with a complete lack of supervision, you can't really relax into your story while you're supposed to be working.

For this reason, imagination-intensive scenes where you need to improvise clever solutions to vexing plot problems will probably be all but impossible to pull off while you're on the clock. If you know you will write at work, consider tackling the scenes you've already mapped out, so you're simply coloring in the predetermined outlines.

3) Never let your novel touch your work computer's hard drive.

Keep your work on a floppy disk or a small "thumb drive" you bring to work with you. This way you won't get confused with multiple versions of the same file, and you'll be able to take it home with you easily at the end of the day and rejoin the bits you wrote with the main document. Also, keeping the file off your computer desktop makes it less likely a snooping boss will stumble across your masterpiece.

Even saving your work on a floppy disk won't completely cover up the tracks of your noveling. The file name and the fact that it originated from the floppy drive will show up in several places on your computer, including the drop-down "recently accessed documents" list on your word processor. Clear your novel file from this list by opening four or five other documents at the end of each day. And you can also make it look less suspicious by naming your novel file something innocuous like "accounts_summary.doc" or "presentation_draft.doc."

4) Be ready to toggle over to a "cover" file at all times.

A few well-timed keystrokes can send you smoothly from your personal document into the work-approved sanctuary of an Excel file. Carole McBay, twenty-six, a three-time NaNoWriMo winner from London, recommends the potent alt-tab combination—which lets you escape to a different program. If you're going to write at work, practice that keystroke at night until you can do it with the stealth and speed of a ninja.

Quirky Places

For twenty-eight-year-old Carolyn Lawrence, a two-time NaNoWriMo winner from Atlanta, the gym emerged as a surprisingly productive place to get work done.

"Treadmills always get my creative juices flowing," she says, laughing. "Though most of the members of the gym now think that there is something seriously wrong with me, because I talked my plot out loud to myself while working out, all while I was wearing my headphones."

However questionable the results can sometimes be, one of the joys of the noveling journey is applying your creativity to some conventionally uncreative spaces. Necessity is truly the mother of invention, and your tight deadline will transform formerly inert waystations into magical writing hubs. Take advantage of off-beat spaces; they can be a great way to keep your word-count high and your imagination stoked.

Oakland's Tim Lohnes, the come-from-behind writer from chapter two, swears by cheap motel rooms as productive places to get writing done (he uses the Web to book last-minute hotel rooms in out-of-the-way suburbs).

A more intoxicating option is to write in your neighborhood pub. Two-time NaNoWriMo winner Amy Probst, thirty-six, of Detroit, Michigan, likes to drag her writing group to a local watering hole called the Senate.

Amy reports: "My fellow Detroit WriMos and I are fond of putting a mess of quarters in the jukebox down at the Senate for mandatory writing until the music stops. It's good for inspiration. The bar has also provided us with incredible characters and dialogue from the regulars."

I've had similar luck with a brewpub in Oakland. Located next to the Oakland Convention Center, the place is a ghost town after the conventioneers head back to their hotels in the evening. While I was a little nervous to show up at a bar as part of a nerdy writing posse (complete with computers), the staff turned out to be all too glad to have us there.

"It's the laptop people!" one waitress would eventually call excitedly whenever we came in. We *did* get some strange looks from regulars at times, but mostly we were happily left alone to stare intently at our laptop screens while sipping our Guinness.

If you're looking for a *truly* anything-goes bar environment, try a hotel bar lounge. The stomping grounds of perpetually overworked

 THE WONDERS OF COFFEE

Ah, sweet caffeine. If you ever needed any proof that coffee was the wonder drug for novelists everywhere, you won't after next month. Whether you French press it, filter brew it, or buy it in steaming cups from your neighborhood coffeemonger, you will be thankful you have buckets of the bean on hand during your noveling adventure.

Scientists who have studied caffeine's effects on humans have discovered that the drug only takes a few minutes to spread to nearly every cell in the body. It's also a natural antidepressant, elevating moods for up to eight hours per cup. And coffee contains antioxidants whose healthful effects rival those produced naturally by the body.

Coffee's history is a novel in its own right: The drink was first served in Ethiopia, where the leaves, not the beans, were brewed as a tea. Eventually the Yemenis got hold of the magic bean juice, and the coffee craze spread throughout the Arab world and beyond. Sort of. The Yemeni rulers forbade the export of unsterilized beans to the outside world, so supplies remained limited until Dutch traders absconded with a sapling in 1616, raising the purloined plant's offspring in Ceylon. Soon thereafter, the Dutch colonies of Java, Sumatra, and Bali were overflowing with coffee beans and java junkies the world over breathed a sigh of ecstatic relief. Over time, the destinies of Haiti, Brazil, and Guatemala have each been radically altered because of their connections to the crop, with the commodity bringing about everything from slave uprisings to political revolutions to utter economic collapse. All part of the rich legacy of brewed novelist-helper that you're sipping today. Bottoms up!

(and perpetually working) business travelers, hotel bars are laptop-friendly, open late, and offer novelists a front-row seat on the kinds of activities that have filled great novels for centuries: nefarious deals, shady alliances, and steamy, illicit affairs—all accompanied by the salty perk of free cocktail nuts.

THE TOOLS OF THE TRADE

Speaking of snacks! There are a few things you'll need to purchase for your upcoming novelist travails. Like any good vacation, half the fun of writing a novel is getting properly outfitted. A month-long noveling trip requires a shopping spree every bit as enjoyable as a jaunt to the Bahamas. And if you pinch pennies, you can get all the high-tech gear, low-tech tools, and copious amounts of treats you'll need for under $35.

The stuff you need falls neatly into two categories: things you can put in your mouth and things you shouldn't. We'll tackle the inedible writing tools first, and then move on to the essential snacks and drinks.

A Notebook

The universe loves novelists. During the novel-prep and book-writing period, you'll watch, delighted, as the cosmos parts to reveal a rich vein of pilferable, copyright-free material explicitly for your noveling use.

A couple will sit down next to you on the bus and proceed to have an argument that you'll use verbatim as a pivotal turning point in your character's love life. Friends will tell a story about an embarrassing, misrouted email at work, and it will inspire an entire subplot. From random graffiti to raccoon-shaped clouds to heavy-metal ballads on the radio, the natural world will be flinging so many novel-appropriate artifacts, phrases, and characters your way that the most difficult thing during your noveling month will not be finding inspiration but fending off an excess of it.

Your notebook, the most powerful apparatus a novelist can own aside from a coffeemaker, is a bucket for catching the downpour of material the universe provides. The notebook you buy should be small enough to fit comfortably into a pocket or purse, and discreet enough for it to be wielded in public without arousing too much suspicion. Avoid brightly colored, spiral-bound notebooks, as they are prone to shedding pages and snagging on clothes.

A Magical Pen

This is the peanut butter to your notebook's jelly, and as with the notebook, it should be somewhere on your person at all times. When picking out your pen, *you must be absolutely sure that you have found the right one.* Don't grab the first ballpoint that catches your eye in the office supply store. The magical pen will be both your conduit of mystery and a documenter of epiphanies. Getting the wrong pen for the job would be a disastrous start to the writing process. Try every pen available, writing phrases like "I am an unstoppable writing dynamo" and "future bad-ass novelist" on the sample pads. After you do this for long enough, one pen candidate will rise above the rest. That enchanted implement is the one that has been slated to help you on your noveling journey.

If your workplace happens to have a broad array of pens on hand, you can save money (and a trip to the stationery store) by picking out a winner from the supply cabinet when no one's looking.

A Word-Processing Device

This is the vast digital warehouse for your novel, and it will likely be the one thing on this list of must-haves that you already own.

Because of their go-anywhere, can-do attitudes, laptop computers are the best tool for the job. If your laptop is somewhat past its prime, you can increase its usefulness as a noveling tool by ordering a new battery (or two) for it from online auction sites, such as Ebay.

Some NaNoWriMo participants swear by an affordable machine called an Alphasmart (www.alphasmart.com). This is a battery-powered, word-processing device that looks like a cross between a laptop and a children's Speak & Spell. The miniscule screen only displays four lines of text or so at a time, which can be helpful in warding off obsessive editing. The keyboard is large and comfortable, and you can work for up to 700 hours on a few AA batteries.

If you're not ready to drop a couple hundred dollars on a new machine, though, don't worry: A desktop computer, PDA with fold-out keyboard, a even a manual typewriter will do fine. Go with whatever you have access to; NaNoWriMo participants have successfully written entire 50,000-word novels using everything from voice-recognition software to a pencil and paper.

A Reference Book

When you start writing, you'll find grammatical and style questions popping up immediately. Are quotes always set off from descriptive text with indents? How do you handle parenthetical comments that are actually stand-alone sentences? Are you supposed to italicize internal monologues?

A professional editor would tell you to pick up a usage guide like William Strunk Jr.'s *The Elements of Style* or, even worse, the *Chicago Manual of Style*. I find both books to be awkwardly laid out and dangerously sleep-inducing. So in the interest of keeping momentum while I write, I keep a copy of Nick Hornby's *High Fidelity* close at hand to use as a template for formatting or style issues. Any book you know and love is a perfect candidate for a reference novel, but this is also a great opportunity to pamper yourself by buying a novel you've been wanting to read for a long time.

Music

Music is the most potent writing drug available without a prescription. Before you start writing, amass as many songs as possible that might be conducive to noveling. Every novel, explicitly or not, has a soundtrack. Finding that soundtrack, and listening to novel and scene-appropriate music as you write, will help you slip into the sensual realms you're describing. Whether you're tapping into the hyperbolic violence of a horror novel or the prim grace of a historical romance, there's some complementary music out there eager to help you get it written.

I'm a big fan of movie scores, as they tend to be overly dramatic in all the right ways. When your character is striding off for the final showdown with the landlord or the face-eating remora, you don't want to have the Bee Gees cooing about dance fevers in the background.

 HEARING VOICES: THE POWER OF HEADPHONES

When writing a novel, I *always* wear large, ear-covering headphones. Sometimes I even remember to plug them into my CD player.

I like wearing headphones because they help dampen the clatter of the outside world without giving me the closed-off, scuba-diver feel that earplugs tend to. And when they're hooked up to a CD or MP3 player, headphones shove the music directly into my brain in beautiful, cinematic ways, adding lovely contours to the rough edges of my thoughts and amplifying my sentences as they come spraying out onto the page.

Headphones, with or without music, also create a social buffer around you. This is especially helpful if you are a woman trying to get your novel written in a cafe. For a certain type of gregarious person (read: man), the sight of someone with a furrowed brow typing madly on a laptop in a public place sends the following very clear message: "I am not working on anything important; please come bother me." Headphones are the perfect foil for keeping these well-meaning, deeply annoying people at bay.

You want the epic rumble of kettle drums and the spiraling scream of an overheated string section. Yaaar!

Whatever your musical predilections, plan on creating loads of energy-bolstering mixes for your writing plunge. Or, if you have a fast Internet connection, take advantage of online radio stations such as Radio Netscape (www.netscape.com), where dozens of genre-specific streams are ready to fulfill your every soundtrack whim.

A Writing Totem

Spider-Man has his tights; Wonder Woman has those bullet-deflecting bracelets. Berkeley's Erin Allday has her fingerless gloves.

"They're a super-cheap pair of black cotton gloves from the Gap," the thirty-year-old, three-time NaNoWriMo winner explains. "All the fingers are uneven because I'm so bad at using scissors. I pretty much have to put them on when I get stuck working on my NaNoWriMo novel. They make me feel so old-school writerly, like I'm some struggling novelist sitting by candlelight in an apartment that I can't afford to keep adequately heated. They definitely put me in the mood to write. It's also a nice tactile distraction, where I'm focused on my fingers and the actual act of typing instead of staying in my head and trying to make the words sound pretty."

As Erin can attest, you are about to spend a month living far above the realm of mere mortals, and you, too, need something you can wear to inspire your superheroic abilities.

A wearable, writing-enhancing object serves several important purposes. First, it helps you transition from the world of everyday living into the fictional realms you've created. In the former you are a normal person, working a normal job. In the latter, you are an all-powerful deity capable of laying waste to entire cities with a few taps of the keyboard.

For me, when I don my plastic Viking helmet, I know I've left the real world behind and am sailing off to the shores of my fictional Valhalla. The hat reminds me that I am Elsewhere, and I will be staying there until the ship's reserves of Dr Pepper and Starburst run low.

Putting on a writing cap, cape, wig, or pantsuit will also serve to remind you that this is a fun, somewhat ridiculous creative exercise, where the goal is to spend a few weeks writing for the hell of it. For some reason, it's hard to overthink your writing when you're wearing a three-foot-tall Marie Antoinette wig.

Personally, I like to have several tiers of headwear, depending on how my story is coming along. If all's well, I'll wear my baseball hat, the ideal thinking cap for sporty, low-exertion writing. The Viking helmet is for the more complicated passages. And if things are going horribly awry in my novel, I bust out my cowboy hat, which I pull down low over my eyes in a menacing fashion to warn my uncooperative story that an unholy dose of hurt is about to be unleashed upon it if it doesn't fall into line.

Conveniently, having something special you wear when you write provides a visual cue to anyone you're living with, including small children, that you've slipped away into the shadowy Realm of the Novel, and that you are not to be disturbed unless they—or one of the more likable of the family pets—are on fire.

EATING YOUR WAY TO 50,000 WORDS

If I had to describe my motivational strategy for drafting a novel in one month, it would be this: treat-o-rama.

Writing a novel is a creative exercise, sure, but it's also a remarkably convenient opportunity to shower yourself with self-love, goodies, and other pampering items you've gone far too long without having in your life. Allowing yourself loads of restaurant meals, sugary treats, and exotic beverages is the best way to keep your spirits high during the exhausting mental acrobatic routines you'll be pulling off next month as you write.

Takeaway Food from Local Restaurants

Month-long novel writing is like running a marathon: You need to make sure you have the right fuel available at all times, preferably handed to you by strangers as you run past them. Thankfully, there are dozens of restaurants in your area that will serve as your nutritional support staff, all for less than $8 per entree.

Avail yourself of the hospitality of these culinary good samaritans during your noveling month. Remember: You have not been put on this Earth to cook meals for yourself *and* write a novel. Delegate the kitchen work as often as possible, and everyone will be the happier for it.

Mass Meals

If you find the takeout meals are starting to drive you into debt, hit the grocery stores and stock up on the fixin's for Mass Meals. These are the easy-to-prepare-in-vast-quantities entrees that you know and love from institutional cafeterias and buffet lines. Consider an acre-sized pan of lasagna, a two-ton casserole, or a vat of tuna salad. Potatoes can be baked by the dozen, then refrigerated until you're ready to top them with cheese and veggies.

Massive Snacks

Speaking of veggies.... When you're writing, you'll eat just about anything that lingers near your keyboard for more than thirty seconds, which makes this an excellent time to get caught up on all those boring vitamin- and mineral-laden foods you spend the rest of the year avoiding.

Go crazy in the produce aisle of your favorite grocer, and buy a ton of carrots, celery sticks, broccoli, green peppers, and anything else that catches your eye. Then take them home, chop 'em up, and leave them in a bowl of water in the fridge. They'll keep longer that way, and they'll also be crisp and cool when you're ready to graze.

A writer cannot live by celery sticks alone, however. As you wrestle with your novel, you'll need the explosive energy bursts that only a steady diet of manufactured sugar can provide. Stockpile chocolate in all its mouth-watering forms.

The only cautionary question you should ask yourself is, "Can I shove these things into my mouth and then type without leaving residue all over the computer?" Some snacks are more keyboard friendly than others.

Once you've accumulated your weight in junk food, you should dispense it according to the following careful criteria: Did you just finish a paragraph? Have a treat.

Drinks

Beverage scientists have discovered that dehydration is one of the main factors in making a person feel tired. As it's all but impossible to work on your novel while you're collapsed over your keyboard asleep, you should constantly pump your body full of fluids while working.

Water, however boring, is a must. But having lots of adventuresome drinks on hand also makes the novel-writing process a little more exciting, with each trip to the refrigerator mirroring your own literary voyage of discovery. So go wild at the grocery store when you stock up, getting both old favorites and some new oddities. Mango-choco-guava nectar? Sure! Pomegranate-beet soda? You bet!

And don't forget to load up on the warm drinks as well. Coffee, tea, and hot chocolate are soothing balms for frazzled synapses. In addition to serving as excellent caffeine conduits, their warmth is physically reassuring, and their slow-sipping properties make them the perfect noveling pause. It also feels wonderfully picturesque and romantic to have a steaming beverage near your computer while you're working, especially if someone is going to be dropping by to see how the writing is going.

CHAPTER 4

Cruising for Characters,
Panning for Plots,
and the First Exciting
Glimpses of the Book Within

After months of preparation, Jennifer McCreedy had an absolutely clear vision of how her intricate fantasy novel would unfurl.

"I churned out character biographies, world maps, and language keys," says the twenty-year-old one-time NaNoWriMo winner from Detroit. "I had developing cultures, societies, religions, hierarchical class structures—even regional clothing, genetic quirks, weapons, and customs."

When the month began, Jennifer dove in with all of her notes at her side—and promptly stopped writing.

"I did so much developmental work on the novel that when it came time to actually write it, I was horrified at what I was coming up with. I'd committed too much to making a complete world for my novel just to watch it crumble under the needs of a November 30th deadline. So I set it aside for future work and started completely anew."

Jennifer's experience echoes the dismay of thousands of National Novel Writing Month participants who have brought months or years of novel ideas to the writing table and ended up finding them to be more of a hindrance than a help in getting something written.

It may be counterintuitive, but when it comes to novel writing, more preparation does not necessarily produce a better book. In fact, too much preparation has a way of stopping novel writing altogether. As reassuring as it is to embark on your writing journey with a mule-team's worth of character traits, backstories, plot twists, metaphors, and motifs, it's also a 100 percent viable strategy to walk into the wilds of your novel with nothing but a bottle of water and a change of underwear.

That said, some amount of planning and predeparture decision-making can be incredibly helpful. And few things in life rival the brainstormy fun of sitting in a coffeeshop with your notebook and pen contemplating the delicious inventory of ideas, people, places, and expressions that might work well in your book. Even if you're going to improvise your plot as you write, it will help in the long run if you ruminate a little on what kinds of things you'd like to write about.

And the planners out there should feel free to completely bury their homes and apartments in plot notes, character lists, story outlines, city maps, costume drawings, evocative photos, and encouraging quotes. All with one catch: You only get one week, maximum, to research your book before you start writing it.

RESEARCH MADE PAINLESS: THE FIVE-CLICK GOOGLE

In doing research for your book, it's easy to get overwhelmed by the enormous amount of things you don't know about your subject. To make sure I don't end up in a whimpering, panicked ball underneath my computer, I've come up with a novel research technique I call the Five-Click Google. Say, for instance, I want to set my upcoming novel in Singapore, and base it around the life of the bartender who invented the Singapore Sling cocktail. I'm not sure why this seems like a good idea, but my heart's set on it.

Do I know anything about Singapore? No. Have I ever consumed a Singapore Sling? Nope.

Great. This is where the Five-Click Google comes in. I bring up the search engine on Google.com and type "Singapore sling," "history," and "Singapore" and hit enter. Now the entirety of my research is to be accomplished in five of the 1,023,009 hits Google has found that match my query.

Thanks to the über-wired nature of the Internet, those five clicks are actually surprisingly bountiful. In less than twenty minutes, I know that the drink was invented in the 1920s by a bartender named Ngiam Ton Boon at the Raffles Hotel in Singapore, and that the drink is a cherry brandy cocktail that sells for an extortionate seventeen dollars. I also learn that the Raffles Hotel was a hot spot for writers in the first few decades of the twentieth century, and that Somerset Maugham haunted the grounds for years, penning odes to the Orient.

A famous writer. An infamous drink. And a coming war that would change their destinies forever. I can hear the voice-over for the movie version of my book already. Thanks, Google!

THE HAPPY SIDE EFFECTS OF LIMITED PLANNING

I know one week seems like a very short amount of time for laying out an entire novel, but trust me: It's perfect. Seven days gives you enough time to get some good ideas on paper, but it prevents the deadly onset of overplanning, which is dangerous for three reasons:

1) If you give yourself too much time to plan, you might end up stumbling across a brilliant concept for your novel. And the last thing you want heading into your noveling month is a brilliant concept. Every year during National Novel Writing Month, I get emails from people jubilantly informing me that they're dropping out of the contest because they've found a story they love, and they want to work on it slowly enough to do it justice.

When I check in with these people six months later, they've inevitably stopped working on the book entirely. Why? Because they've become afraid of ruining their book by actually sitting down and writing it.

A novel rough draft is like bread dough; you need to beat the crap out of it for it to rise. Once you stumble across a fantastic, once-in-a-lifetime idea for a book, it's hard to treat that story with the irreverent disregard needed to transform it from a great idea into a workable rough draft. When you just give yourself one week to flesh out your concept, you won't have time to feel overly protective of your ideas. And you will therefore stand a much better chance of bringing them to life.

2) Past a certain point, novel planning just becomes another excuse to put off novel writing. You will *never* feel sufficiently ready to jump into your novel, and the more time you spend planning and researching, the more likely you'll feel pressure to pull off a masterwork that justifies all your prewriting work. Give yourself the gift of a pressure-free novel, and just dive in after one week.

3) Prewriting, especially if you're very good at it, bleeds some of the fun out of the noveling process. Nothing is more boring than spending an entire month simply inking over a drawing you penciled out months earlier. With the seven-days-and-out timeline, you'll still have lots of questions about your book when you start writing. Which is great. It makes the writing process one of happy discoveries and keeps the levels of surprise and delight high for you as an author.

So as you look over the gaggle of questions about character, plot, setting, and language in the rest of this chapter, know that they are by no means meant as a rigorous checklist to be completed before starting your novel. They're just a way to help you figure out what you love in novels, and by extension, what you might like to put in yours.

THE TWO MAGNA CARTAS

Let's start our discussion of your book with a quick exercise.

Using your noveling notebook and pen of wonder, jot down answers to the following question: What, to you, makes a good novel?

It's an excruciatingly broad question, but give it a shot. And feel free to be as vague or as nerdily detailed as you like; this list can include anything from ultra-short chapters to ribald sex scenes to massive infusions of ill-tempered elves. Anything that floats your fictional boat should go on the list.

My list, to help give you some ideas, looks like this:

- first-person narration
- quirky characters
- true love
- found objects
- disappointment
- music
- catharsis
- feisty old people
- strong, charismatic protagonists
- improbable romances
- smart but unpretentious writing
- urban settings
- cliffhanger chapter endings
- characters who are at turning points in their lives
- books set in the workplace
- happy endings

Okay, now make your list. Go crazy, and take as long as you want.

Once you've finished, frame it. This document will be your Magna Carta for the next month, helping you channel your awesome writing powers for the good of the people.

Why is this list so frame-worthy?

Because the things that you appreciate as a reader are also the things you'll likely excel at as a writer. These bits of language, color, and technique, for whatever reason, make sense to your creative brain. These are the Things You Understand. And as you draw the basic outlines of your novel over the next week, you should to try to fill that outline in with as many of the juicy elements from the Magna Carta as possible.

If you like it when authors start chapters with quotations, for instance, start gathering some pithy zingers for your story. Are coming-of-age tales your guilty pleasure? Consider setting your story at a summer camp. The chances are good that if a mood, motif, or plot device resonates with you as a reader, you'll be able to adeptly wield it when you're in the writer's seat as well.

Okay, that's the first list. Now on to its equally important sibling . . .

For the second list, write down those things that bore or depress you in novels. Again, feel free to be as specific or wide-ranging as you like. And be honest. If you don't like books where the words-to-pictures ratio favors the text too heavily, write that down. We're not here to judge. We just want to understand you better.

My list would include the following:

- irredeemably malicious main characters
- books set on farms
- mentally ill main characters
- food or eating as a central theme
- ghosts, monsters, or demons

| dysfunctional sibling dramas |
| books consisting largely of a character's thoughts |
| weighty moral themes |
| books set in the nineteenth century |
| unhappy endings |

Now it's your turn. Write down anything and everything that bores you or brings you down in a book. Go.

When you're finished, frame this list as well. We'll call it Magna Carta II, the Evil Twin of Magna Carta I.

As you spend the next week thinking about what you want to have in your novel, keep MCII close at hand, so you'll remind yourself what *not* to put in your story.

I know it seems silly to have to remind yourself to keep things you dislike out of your novel, but be warned: The stealthy entries on your MCII list are vicious, cunning little buggers, and given the slightest opening, they *will* find their way into your book.

The reason they'll make their way onto your pages is related to the same scientific principle of self-betterment that causes us to bring high-brow tomes home from the bookstore knowing full well they'll go straight onto the bookshelf and never be touched again until our kids move us and our possessions into that miserable senior home down the road.

We buy these difficult books because we feel that, while not very exciting, they are in some way *good* for us. It's a sort of literature-as-bran-flake philosophy: If something is dry and unpalatable, it must be doing something good to our constitutions. This kind of thinking also carries over to the writing realm. If we're worried that our story is lacking in substance, the first thing most of us automatically reach for to fix it are the bran morsels from the MCII.

Still not convinced? Let me offer a real-world example.

When sitting down to craft my second month-long novel, I decided that my previous work—a story about an American music nerd secretly in love with his Scottish green-card wife—had been high on fluff and low on substance.

I was right. So, on my second work, I committed myself to writing a Serious Book. Lacking any appropriately substantial ideas, I simply saddled an otherwise enjoyable main character with an ever-lengthening roster of mental illnesses, suicidal relatives, and ghosts, handily crushing the protagonist's spirit under the pressure of weighty moral themes.

In my quest for writing that would last for generations, I managed to write a book that wore out its welcome in less than three days. Having packed almost every single item on my MCII list into one overwrought package, I lost interest in the main character and her morose life after about 5,000 words, and it was just out of sheer stubbornness, force of will, and a terrifying dearth of any other plausible novel ideas that I was able to see the book through to its predictably depressing finale.

The lesson here is this: If you won't enjoy reading it, you won't enjoy writing it. If you truly are fascinated by the plight of the nation's mentally ill, the ongoing politicization of religious sects in Saudi Arabia, or inner city high-rise housing projects as metaphors for racial injustice and miscarried modernization, by all means put them in your book.

But if, in your heart of hearts, you really want to write a book about a pair of super-powered, kung-fu koalas who wear pink capes and race through the city streets on miniature go-karts, know that this is also a wonderful and completely valid subject for a novel.

As you plan your book this week, remember, above all else, that your novel is not a self-improvement campaign. Your novel is a spastic, jubilant hoe-down set to your favorite music, a thirty-day visit to a candy store where everything is free and nothing is fattening. When thinking about possible inclusions for your novel, always grab the guilty pleasures over the bran flakes. Write your joy, and good things will follow.

THE PREWRITING PARADE: NANOWRIMO WINNERS SHARE THEIR TIPS ON STORY RESEARCH.

"I'm the king of random input. I read all of my character's horoscopes and run their biorhythms. I draw cards from Trivial Pursuit and force myself to incorporate the answers on the back, I click the random button on LiveJournal."
—Irfon Ahmad, 32, two-time NaNoWriMo winner from Toronto

"During the month, if I needed to know something that would take more than fifteen minutes to look up, I just made it up and wrote in ALL CAPS to signal during the editing that I needed to get the actual information."
—Michele Marques, 39, one-time NaNoWriMo winner from Toronto

"As tempting as it may be to insert historical figures, characters from other stories, or actual facts in your novel, don't do it unless you have an encyclopedic knowledge of the topic in question. Failing that, having a certain looseness of clarity can bail you out of some fairly tricky situations."
—Andrew Johnson, 29, three-time NaNoWriMo winner from Christchurch, New Zealand

"I make scene notes on index cards, using color to separate what characters are involved, or what kind of plot thing is going to happen, and spend the last week in October laying them out like tarot and studying and rearranging them. That way I can see holes in my plot. Once November starts, I can look at a card and know basically what has to happen in the next scene—very good for those moments when I have absolutely no inspiration. Cards enable me to keep slogging. But I only plot through about three quarters of the book—I need some suspense to keep me interested in what's going to happen."
—Suzy Rogers, 46, two-time NaNoWriMo winner from St. Paul, Minnesota

"For my novel, which I realized early on was going to have subplots galore, I not only made an outline (actually lots of outlines), I made a timeline as well. But not a wimpy computer timeline or something sketched on an eight-and-a-half-by-eleven piece of paper. No, I got my boyfriend to bring home a piece of butcher paper, and I made a HUGE timeline that covers my entire bedroom wall. I think starting out with a lot of clear outlines really helped me. It served as a bird's-eye view of the entire novel."
—Michelle Booher, 24, one-time NaNoWriMo winner from Alameda, California

YOUR BOOK
IN TEN QUESTIONS OR LESS

The gilded MCI and dreaded MCII have provided you with a personalized list of noveling Dos and Don'ts. Now it's time to put these insights to use in thinking about your story and its characters, plot, setting, and point of view.

The following discussions are meant solely to help guide you as you ponder the sweet mysteries of your book in the coming week. Brainstorm, make lists, and give every silly idea that occurs to you a chance to make a case for why it should be in your book. After a week of mulling, massing, and discarding, you will have a few book ideas you love and a handful of others you can live with. And then the fun will begin.

Shady Characters

Whether you noticed or not, from the minute you decided to write a novel in a month, the Central Casting wing of your imagination began contemplating contenders for the dramatis personae. Over the next week, you'll start seeing friends and strangers in a different, more apprising light. From the muttering, pimply florist who sells tulips in front of the grocery store to the executive who talks in hushed tones about her evening's sexual conquests on the subway ride to work, the personality traits, quirks, and annoyances of those around you will suddenly be transformed into rich potential fodder for your novel.

But with the huge number of possible characters vying for a role in your book, how do you know who should get the part?

Your Magna Carta I is a great place to start. Looking over my list, I would be wise to keep my eyes peeled for a main character who lives in an urban setting, has a quirky job (maybe working with feisty old people?), and tends to be hopelessly entangled in a quest for true love. (In fact, this describes the main characters in half the books I've written.)

But another great rule for choosing good characters is to simply pick people you would enjoy getting to know better. Remember: You will be spending *a lot* of time with these people. As you consider a possible character for your story, ask yourself this question: How would you feel about going on a month-long cruise with them? Even the unsavory characters in your book—the black-hearted villains and nine-headed gorgons—should be interesting enough that you wouldn't mind playing shuffleboard or sharing the lobster buffet with them every day for a month.

And once you've decided you're going to invite someone onboard your noveling vacation, sit them down with a Mai Tai on the poop deck and ask them as many questions as you can cram into your seven allotted research days. Some good questions include the following:

How old are they?

In some ways, a character's age will decide the timbre of your story, and each age comes with its own set of desires, dreams, challenges, and financial realities. The "write what you know" contingent would probably advise that you only have characters your age or younger. I'm in the "write what you'd like to know more about" camp, so I say the life cycle's the limit. It's true, however, that it will be easier for you to write characters who are close to your current age.

What is their gender?

Writing across gender lines (meaning male authors have female lead characters, and vice versa) is a snap for some people and completely untenable for others. If you're not sure what sex you want your main character/s to be, I'd recommend writing your novel from your own sex's standpoint. This is especially true if this is your first novel.

Once you decide on their sex, begin thinking of ways you can plumb it for plot wrinkles or juicy potential conflicts. If your character is female, where does she depart from traditional notions of femininity? If your character is a man, is he stereotypically male? Or does he cry at commercials featuring babies and kittens?

What do they do for work?

If your character is between the ages of eighteen and sixty-five, he or she is likely going to spend a vast portion of the novel at work. Whether you depict their time on the clock is up to you. As I mentioned in my Magna Carta list, I *love* to fill my novels with the weird goings-on at offices and workplaces. Jobs are places where people who have no business ever meeting spend more time together than most married couples, making work an ideal hotbed for plot-generating alliances, rivalries, and schemes.

Who are their friends, family, and love interests?

The more close friends and nearby family a character has, the more material you'll have for your book. But a larger social circle also means more work for you as a writer (this is especially true if your character has children living at home). Because I am a lazy novelist who gets overwhelmed when I have to juggle more than a couple of characters, I am a sucker for protagonists who have just ended a relationship (instant emotional resonance!) and who have recently moved to a new place (blank social slate!).

More imaginative writers can be a little more ambitious in their cast, but my one big piece of advice for first-time authors is this: Keep it simple. Fifty thousand words will come *much* faster than you think; getting bogged down in a long digression about the protagonist's second-cousins will give you less time to focus on the meat of your book.

What is their living space like?

This question isn't about general location, which we'll discuss under "setting" on page 97, but about the inside of a character's apartment, kitchen, or bedroom. The way people organize their home often mirrors the way they organize their life, and descriptions of the microcosm of the homefront are often nicely subtle ways to flesh out each character's likes, dislikes, and neuroses.

What are their hobbies?

I love afflicting my characters with a wealth of strange pastimes, from arcane collecting manias to participation in obsolete and pathetic sports. What do your characters do when they're not at work? And who do they meet while doing it? Are they on a team? Part of an Internet chat group? What attracts them to the hobbies they do have, and how much time do they give over to recreational pursuits?

What were they doing a year ago? Five years ago?

This is where we get into the nebulous world of "backstory"— the things that happened to the characters before the book began. Some characters are entirely consumed by something—a murder, a breakup, a misplaced winning lottery ticket—that continues to haunt the rest of their lives. You may or may not choose to allude to these things in the book, but knowing what a few of them are will help give you a deeper understanding of your character.

Because I have trouble enough coming up with a front story before I write, I usually let various backstories emerge during the writing process. If you already have some pretty well-defined characters, you could start delving into backstory now: What did they think they were going to be when they grew up? Did they go to their high school prom? Who in their life has had the biggest influence on them? Has their life turned out not quite the way they had expected?

What are their values and politics?

Your characters' ideologies and politics will probably rarely come up directly in the novel, but slipping some telling reactions into the book's background can help flesh out each character's personality. Questions you can ask might include: How would your characters respond to being asked for change by a homeless person? When was the last time they went to church? How do they feel about violent movies?

Hatching Your Plot

This is the biggie. If there's one thing that keeps most people from diving into novel writing, it's an absence of the mysterious thing called plot.

As intimidating as it seems, plot is simply the movement of your characters through time and over the course of your book. Which means that by having characters in your book, you're guaranteed to have a plot. The plot may be subtle, or it may be the kind of thing that causes people to walk into trees because they couldn't put your book down. It's up to you.

Some writers are dazzlingly adept at coming up with the series of unexpected developments and juicy revelations that we commonly regard as a story's plot. If you are one of these people, you are lucky indeed, and the chances are good that you already have a semicomplete story arc in mind for next month's project.

If you do already have a sense of your plot, I recommend you spend as much time as possible "pitching" it to yourself before writing. Talk through the story from start to finish, as if you were laying it out for a particularly patient agent or producer. Be sure to explain the climaxes and the highlights, and try to add a couple of minutes onto your pitch with each retelling.

For the rest of us, the great majority who are unsure of what exactly will, or should, be happening to our characters next month, I say this: Fear not. No plot truly is no problem. The act of writing is a 100 percent reliable plot-forge. It may seem a little scary to leave your story's backbone to chance, but fusing character and setting into an engaging, readable narrative is what our imaginations are best at. Just focus on creating vivid, enjoyable characters, and a plot will unfold naturally from their actions. As I discovered the first time out, characters will eventually *demand* that certain actions be taken, and there's something uniquely thrilling in that moment when you see them take charge.

However, you *can* help the plot percolation process along by taking another gander at your Magna Carta I list. What of the story-oriented items from that list seem most exciting to you as a writer? And which of the things you love would lend themselves well to a short-term novel-writing feast?

Also, if you already have an idea of your characters, you can help sketch out the first plot points by taking some time to think about the dramatic changes, turning points, or horrible events you could inflict on your characters over the course of the book.

Here are some time-tested plot-providers to consider: Can someone in your story get fired? Can a marriage or relationship implode? Can someone get a disease? Can someone die? Can an unexpected windfall occur? Can someone be wronged, and set out to exact vengeance? Can someone find a precious or unusual object? Can your character set off on an impossible quest or journey? Can someone try to become something they're not? Can someone fall in love with someone who is off-limits or wildly inappropriate? Can your character be mistaken for someone else?

If all of these questions sound suspiciously familiar, it's because one of them (coupled with the all-important "What would happen if we added an orangutan to the mix?") has driven the plot of nearly every movie you've ever watched and every book you've ever read.

Some might bemoan the fact that world's plots can be distilled into a quarter page's worth of cliches, but I see it as just further proof of the miraculous power of well-told stories. No matter how many times we hear tales of a pluckish underdog triumphing over an all-powerful foe, we still respond to it. Ditto for romantic comedies. Even when the endings are obvious, we usually don't care so long as the story is well told, with protagonists we can love and antagonists we can throw things at—and with the details grounded in the particulars of their lives and situations.

Which is yet another reason why you shouldn't beat yourself up trying to develop an exciting or original plot in the next seven days. A good plot is less a matter of innovation and invention as it is one of creative re-use; the most acclaimed books of the modern era have used the same building blocks as the worst soap operas and clumsiest cartoons. The main thing separating the mind-blowing, life-changing stories of a great novel from the treacly dreck of daytime TV is the manner in which the tale is told. And this telling is the very thing that will emerge out of the clang and sweat of your weekly blacksmithing next month.

Besides, just because a plot idea heading into your novel feels hackneyed doesn't mean the resulting book will be. As you write your rough draft, the story will take itself in directions you'd never intended. What starts out as a word-for-word re-write of *Jurassic Park* may end up as a historical dramedy set in a Portuguese barber's underpants. It's just the way writing works. Just when you think you know where it's going, it zooms off in a new, unpredicted direction. Don't get me wrong: The quest for originality is an admirable one, and it's something you should definitely think about when you rewrite your manuscripts. For now, though, grab whatever tropes or cliches appeal to you and *go*. You'll be surprised at the quirky plot twists and inspired characters you come up with when you stop worrying so much about being innovative.

Background on Backdrops

Happily, most novel ideas suggest their own settings. A story about rampaging zombies terrorizing a Phish concert, for instance, would best be set in a medium-sized town—the cemetery in a small town probably wouldn't be able to produce enough zombies, and a big city would have too sizable a zombie-repelling security force. Or if you're writing a quirky romance about two people who meet on an online dating service for agoraphobics, most of your story will occur inside apartments, with an occasional miniscule restaurant or airless bar thrown in for nights on the town.

In my experience, the trick of drafting a setting for your novel is in *modeling*. The more you can base the cemeteries, amphitheaters, and claustrophobic restaurants on real-life versions of those things, the more mental energy you'll have for the truly important aspects of writing—eating the chocolate reserves you've stockpiled, bragging about your progress to attractive strangers at parties, and demanding wrist massages from loved ones.

If possible, set your story in the area where you currently reside. If setting the book on familiar turf is not an option, consider having your story take place somewhere you've always wanted to go. This will make writing your novel a little like a vacation, but without all the ragged hours spent stuck in airports. And if you're planning on inventing an entirely new fantasy world for your characters to frolic in, consider drawing out a basic map of the area before you start the actual writing. Improperly routing your orcs to the swampy Scarr of Bectkdor when they should be advancing on the foreboding Mountains of Mignal can cause no end of headaches in the rewrite period.

Wherever you end up setting your story, don't worry overly much about lending an enormous amount of realistic detail to the tale's backdrop. In the same way that a theater set will use two or three potted trees to suggest a forest, so should you leave much of your setting to the reader's imagination in the first draft. The editing stage will be the time to painstakingly fill in all of the parks, bars, and stores that make up your fictional world. With writing time in short supply, it's important to scrimp on the small stuff so you can get the overall gist of the story down before crossing the finish line.

When your story takes place will also have a pretty profound effect on the amount of carpentry work required when preparing your novel's sets. Setting your book in the past or future will require more mental energy than ones where you can borrow the cultural mores, architecture, and technological topography of the present.

If you do decide to set your book in the past or future, be sure to use the same half-assed approach to getting the details right as you would with any aspect of the setting. Having the historically appropriate wool weave on your nineteenth-century character's kneesocks, or detailing the quantum physics powering your twenty-third-century Starhopper, should always take a backseat to getting the basics of your story written.

FAQs on POVs

Though it's the last thing we discuss in this chapter, point of view is the first writerly decision a book reveals to readers. As you think about your characters, you also need to think about the perspective you'll be using to detail their exploits. You essentially have two choices: first person or third person.

Most of you probably remember discussions of first and third person from seventh-grade English classes. In case you're a little rusty, the best way to understand the difference is to think of your story as a movie. In first-person stories, the movie is shot through a single camera glued to the space between your main character's eyebrows. In third person, you get to use as many cameras as you like, and you

FINDING INSPIRATION IN THE WEIRDEST PLACES

From the manicurist to the online personals, NaNoWriMo winners talk about the inspiration behind their novels' people and places.

"I set my 2003 NaNo novel at the Hand Stand, the salon where I get my nails done. I told Ann, the owner, and Terrie, my manicurist, that I was so inspired by them that I was going to shamelessly use them as the main characters in my mystery novel, *The Hand Job*. They were thrilled. I gave Terrie the enviously delicate ankles she had always dreamed of. Ann just wanted to be forty pounds lighter and get a chance to seduce the UPS man, on whom she has had a long-time crush."
—Kimberli Munkres, 37, three-time NaNoWriMo winner from Redlands, California

"I've found that a good place to generate character names is from the glossary in my college physics textbook. I also keep lists of good spam email names in preparation for my next novel. Bradford Martini, Elden Yo, and Vallie Shankles, I *will* write a novel about you."
—Kara Platoni, 28, three-time NaNoWriMo winner from Oakland, California

"Since a character in my story had a dog, I found it helpful to follow someone walking his dog as he ran various errands, and make up their story. I wonder if there are people in my neighborhood who are still trying to avoid me as a stalker?"
—Ryan Dunsmuir, 38, five-time NaNoWriMo winner from Brooklyn

"One year I decided to write about polyamorous couples—people who engage in loving and open multiperson relationships. In order to research their world, I checked out a Web site devoted to matching such people with like-minded couples. The only problem was that in order to see all the profiles, I had to write one myself. So I was forced to go undercover as a neophyte bisexual looking for a caring, nonpagan, somewhat hip, somewhat slim couple from the San Francisco area. Sadly, no one ever contacted me."
—Dan Strachota, 35, five-time NaNoWriMo winner from San Francisco

can place them anywhere, from the bottom of a blimp passing over the city to an ant hiking up your character's shoe.

The first-person perspective is immediately comfortable for first-time novelists because it echoes the language we use when telling stories in conversations, emails, letters, and journal entries. It's also very conducive to high-speed noveling, since you can spend as much time as you like paddling around in the bottomless depths of a character's thoughts.

If you are writing in an "I"-based narration style, though, know that you will be trapped in one body for the whole story. Ultimately, what this means is that if your main character wants to leave a party just as you're starting to enjoy yourself, you have to go home as well. When your character wants to take a nap, the story stops. And if something essential happens while they're in the bathroom, you'll miss it.

Going with third person, on the other hand, lets you see all of the action, regardless of how long your characters spend in the bathroom. In third-person point of view, the characters, all of whom are described as "he" or "she," are more or less interchangeable from a narrative perspective.

Third person gives you the power of monitoring the words, actions, and thoughts of everyone in a scene. With the third-person perspective, you are able to peer into every nook and cranny of your fictional realm, and everything can be revealed to the reader.

If that sounds like a clear argument for third-person point of view, remember that with the added number of perspectives comes increased responsibility. If you have the ability of showing *everything*, you're forced to spend a lot more time separating the essential from the superfluous. Also, you'll have to worry about hurt feelings and an unbalanced storyline if you start playing favorites and giving more book time to one character over another. With first person, the field of view is reduced, but that limitation means less running around for you as the writer.

Ultimately both POVs are great, and you'll just need to decide which works best with the tone of your story. And you don't need to commit to just one: Feel free to play around with first and third person as you go, letting different characters tell their sides of the story. Sometimes handing the narration over to a different character can save both story and author when things in the book hit a difficult point.

And yes, there is something called second-person point of view. It looks like this: "You sense that the author has begun using an odd, second-person narration style. It feels unnatural and awkward, and it reminds you of those Choose-Your-Own-Adventure novels you read in fourth grade."

You are not allowed to use second-person perspective in your novel next month. Not even ironically. Sorry. Rules are rules.

SECTION TWO*

Write Here!

Write Now!

A Frantic, Fantastic

Week-by-Week Overview

to Bashing out Your Book

*For maximum effect, read each of the following four chapters at the beginning of
their corresponding weeks. Also, no skipping ahead! Peeking at Week Two's pep talk
while you're still exploring the exciting terrain of Week One will cause strange
and disquieting rifts in the temporal fabric of the universe, and may needlessly
jeopardize the lives of everyone on this planet. Be a responsible (and fiendishly
creative) global citizen and take the chapters one week at a time.

CHAPTER 5

WEEK ONE:

Trumpets Blaring, Angels Singing, and Triumph on the Wind

Dear Writer,

Here it is: Day One. We're standing together on the precipice that overlooks the vast, uncharted territory of your novel. It's quite a view.

Every author you've ever admired started out at this same point, gazed out with the same mix of wonder and trepidation at that small, verdant speck on the horizon called The End. You are ready, poised. The sun is shining, the birds are singing, and there's an unmistakable smell of victory in the air.

There's also an unmistakable smell of hot dogs wafting over from the Noveling Viewing Platform Snack Shop in the main parking lot.

They're running a two-for-one special today, and if you didn't pack a lunch for the trip, I tell you: Get the cheddarwurst.

Mmmm . . . victory and hot dogs. Does life get any sweeter?

It just might.

For, in a matter of minutes, you'll be setting out on your great noveling adventure. As unbelievable as it may seem, in just one month's time you will have written a book the size of the one you are now holding. On the path to noveldom, you'll ford rushing rivers of adversity, and repel countless attacks by television shows, movies, Internet chat rooms, and other bewitching distractions as you hack tirelessly through brambly questions of character, plot, and setting

At the end of it all, you'll stand on that faraway, majestic peak, manuscript clutched to your monitor-irradiated chest, your sore, swollen arms raised in a gesture of total literary triumph.

The lessons you take from your travels across novel-land this month will serve you well throughout the rest of your life. You will walk away from the four-week escapade with a mischievous sense of boldness and an increased confidence in your creative abilities. You will read differently, and write differently, and for better or worse, you will begin seeing the world with the ever-hungry eyes of a novelist.

And before you set off on your valiant and overcaffeinated mission, there's one thing I'll need to take from you.

I'll need to confiscate your Inner Editor.

That's right, the Inner Editor. The doubting, self-critical voice that we all inherited around puberty as an unfortunate door prize for surviving childhood. The Inner Editor is a busybody and perfectionist, happiest when it's tsk-tsking our shortcomings and weaving our past blunders into a rich tapestry of personal failure.

For reasons not entirely clear to anyone, we invite this fun-spoiling tyrant along with us on all our artistic endeavors. And from painting to music-making to writing, our endeavors have paid the price of this killjoy's presence. Thanks to the Inner Editor's merciless second-guessing, most of our artistic output ends up tentative and truncated, doomed to be abandoned at the first sign that the results are anything short of brilliant.

The fear of doing things imperfectly turns what should be fun, creative endeavors into worrisome tasks. With the Inner Editor on board, completing any extracurricular activity you haven't already mastered is like trying to ride a bicycle uphill while towing a rhinoceros in a wagon behind you.

This month, we lose the rhino.

Because this month, you'll leave your Inner Editor here with me at the fully licensed, board-certified *No Plot? No Problem!* Inner Editor Kennel—where it can spend its days carping with other Inner Editors, happily pointing out typos in the newspaper and complaining about the numerous plot holes on daytime television.

It will be very, very happy here.

And you can have the beastie back in a month's time, after you've written your book. Your Inner Editor, despite its incompatibility with

 TIMING IS EVERYTHING: OPTIMIZING YOUR NOVELING TIME BY FINDING YOUR GOLDEN HOURS

One of the greatest lessons you'll learn over the next four weeks is that it's possible to churn out inspired prose regardless of how tired and unhappy you are when you sit down to write.

That said, everyone has certain hours of the day where the brain is just better-oiled than others. Finding out when these juicy hours fall, and spending as much time at the keyboard during them, will offer a tremendous boost to your book. These golden hours vary from person to person: Mine happen to run from about 9:00 A.M., when the coffee first hits, to 1:00 P.M., when all I want to do is crawl under my desk and fall asleep. If your most alert, creative hours occur in the morning (while you're at work or school), you can still make a point of exploiting them on weekends. Ditto for the night owls who just start hitting their stride around 3:00 A.M.

And whenever you have an especially challenging scene to write, try putting it off until you can have a go at it from within your golden hours' friendly synaptic confines.

rough drafts, is the perfect companion in the rewrite process. Because at that point, you will be giving it enough big-picture work to do that it won't have the time or energy to exhaust you with nitpicky comments about every comma and contraction.

So here's the deal I'm proposing: I'll take that heavy, anxious Inner Editor off your hands for four weeks. No charge. And in exchange, you promise to write your novel in a high-velocity, take-no-prisoners, anything-goes style that would absolutely horrify it.

All you need to do is touch the "Take My Inner Editor" button below, and a small, invisible team of humane, editor-removal specialists will be dispatched from the spine of this book to collect the thing for the kennel.

Since your Inner Editor will be led away within a few seconds of you pressing the button, don't touch it until you're ready. Take a few moments if you need to. Once your Inner Editor is safely in our kennels (and well out of earshot), we'll run through the last few things you need to know before setting out on your trip.

TAKE MY INNER EDITOR

Okay, with that behind us, let's get ready to go. I have just three final requests before we get started.

1) Please take this challenge very seriously.

You've signed the Month-Long Novelist Agreement and Statement of Understanding. Now see it through. Set regular writing goals, and stick to them. Your brain may be telling you it's time to turn off the computer and go to bed. But the human brain, if left to its own devices, would spend its entire adult life napping in front of the television. Ignore your brain. Toughen up. Keep your butt in that chair until you've bagged the day's quota. It's the only way you'll ever survive to see the finish line.

2) Do not take any of this very seriously.

Writing a novel in a month is utterly ridiculous, an undertaking for fools and those who don't know any better. Thankfully, we belong to the latter camp, which makes us dangerously powerful writers. Liberated from the constraints of constructing a pretty and proper novel, we are free to run, naked and whooping, through the valleys of our imaginations.

This month, your story will achieve an at-times frightening force and velocity. Go with it. Write wildly, joyfully, in huge and bounding strokes. Was that last page the worst thing you've ever written? Maybe. Does it matter? Nope. All words are good words this month. Follow tangents. Change directions at will. Stay loose. Make messes. Laugh at it all. You are doing something weird and wonderful here, and none of it will go on your permanent record.

3) Know that you have done all of this before.

A novel is just a story that's been bound. If there's one thing humans excel at, it's telling tales. Our narrative voices have been honed through years of conversation, letters, and gossipy emails. We know how to string audiences along, slowly deploying just enough of the juicy bits to keep them hanging. The ability to braid together life experiences in a compelling way is part of our birthright.

Throughout the month, you'll find yourself drawing on strengths and abilities you didn't realize you possessed. There will be excruciatingly difficult days, sure. But the skills and tools to get you through the hard times are already within you. You've been writing a novel your whole life. This month is just the time when you finally get it down on paper.

Okay, let's do a final check, and then you're ready to head off.

THOUGHTS FROM THE TRENCHES: NANOWRIMO WINNERS ON THE FIRST DAYS OF THE ADVENTURE

"The best thing about Week One is that it's all there, baby, a big wide world for me to create. It could go anywhere. The worst thing is that there are too many different directions that I could go, and I get hung up on picking the 'right' one."
—Cybele May, 37, three-time NaNoWriMo winner from Los Angeles

"The best thing about the first week for me is the energy I get from being able to finally write something specific after holding back for the month (or at least the few weeks) before the contest starts. The worst part is the week just before NaNo starts, when I'm absolutely convinced that all the ideas that have been bouncing around in my head will completely disappear, and I'll be left looking like an idiot, unable to string a coherent sentence together if my life depended on it."
—Michael Sirois, 57, one-time NaNoWriMo winner from Houston, Texas

"Week One is when the bad-idea naps start happening. At first, I had this notion that a good power nap early in the evening would give you a formidable burst of writing energy later. Instead, what it gives you is an accidental good night's sleep."
—Brian Baldi, 30, one-time NaNoWriMo winner from Amherst, Massachusetts

"The first week, like the weeks after it, is analogous to age. The first ten thousand words are like your first decade on Earth, flying by in a rush. The second ten grand is like adolescence—full of high highs and low lows, all awkward and gangly and manic. The twenty to thirty period is one of confusion and uncertainty, when you're trying to figure out what you want to be. From thirty- to forty-thousand, you get a bit sad: Suddenly you see what you have and there's no turning back and you've got to play out your hand. The last ten thousand is a total breeze, as you see the finish line and you're just wrapping things up. Then you die."
—Dan Strachota, 35, five-time NaNoWriMo winner from San Francisco

Do you have:

- A magical writing totem or two?
- Your reference book?
- Music to write to?
- Snacks, drinks, and luxury pampering supplies?

Then you're ready to go. Take a deep breath, head over to that word-processing device, and turn it on.

I think there's a novel that's been waiting a long time to meet you.

WEEK ONE ISSUES

At the start of each week, we'll take a look at some of the time-specific hurdles, junctions, and waystations that you'll be passing during those seven days on your way to 50,000 words. This week, we'll look at the conundrums related to the first sentence, the first time you save your manuscript, and the end of the first chapter.

It Was the Best of Times, It Was the Worst of Times: Writing the Ideal First Sentence

The first sentence is, in many ways, a perfect microcosm of your novel. Meaning you're probably worrying way too much about it.

Your first sentence does not need to reflect the dynamic character of your novel. It is not an oracle or bellwether for how well the month will go, nor is it a predictor of the beautiful or horrendous prose that will follow it. It's simply a friendly announcement from your fingers to your brain that it best stop working on other things and get its butt down to your novel.

In this way, your first sentence is really just a set of chimes decorating the door of your novel, more of a ceremonial marker of a threshold than any sort of purposeful item. So go ahead and start the book off with whatever out-of-left-field image or statement occurs to you.

In my novels, I like to start with something storytelly to loosen my mental muscles. Past erudite winners have included: "Okay, the story starts like this . . . " Or, "Crap. Time to start the novel. Okay, well, I guess it opens on . . . " Or, most originally, "Once upon a time . . . "

At some point, your first sentence will be reshaped into a beautifully inviting calling card for your book. Happily, that time is still at least a month away. For now you should go with whatever strikes your fancy.

The Name on the E-Birth Certificate:
The First Save

The second big challenge of the month will come a few paragraphs after you solve the opening-sentence dilemma—when you have to save your document for the first time, and you are suddenly confronted by the impersonal archivist of your word-processing program demanding that the book have a name.

If you already have a title, you're golden. But if you only have a working title (or, more likely, no title at all), you may find yourself a little panicked at the prospect of having to choose a name this early in the process.

Since I always have trouble coming up with titles that feel appropriate or significant or even vaguely related to the unfolding book, I tend to call my files "award_winning_masterpiece.doc" or "dumb_book_number_two.doc" or something similarly nondescript. And when I finally come up with a title I like (usually around Week Three), I'll do a Save As at the end of a writing session and—with much ceremonial toasting, bubble gum–cigar chewing, and dancing in the office chair—christen the novel with its new name.

NO PLOT? NO PROBLEM!

Knowing When to Bring the Curtains Down:
Ending Chapters

As you write this week, you will likely come up against another very good initial question. Namely: When am I supposed to end a chapter?

Some sections contain clear cut-points—a character going to bed, for example, or stepping in front of a bus—but early in the writing process, when you're not exactly sure where your story is headed, your chapters are bound to be lopsided and distinctly unchapterlike, with some going on for thirty pages and others barely managing to last to the end of the first sentence.

This is a-okay. Later in the month you'll begin carving out well-paced, evenly allocated chapters as you find your book's rhythm. For now, you can't have too many or too few, so chapter-ize at will, captain.

WEEK ONE TIPS

Throughout the next four chapters, we'll also take a look at some strategies that will come in especially handy in dealing with each week's particular challenges. Week One's tips center on leveraging the adrenaline rush of the first few days, avoiding the pernicious desire to self-edit as you write, creating a convenient home for your castaway thoughts, and maintaining momentum by keeping your story a mystery to those around you.

Ride the Momentum

The first week of writing is an explosively productive creative period. With good reason. Your imagination, consigned to enjoying and analyzing other people's creative efforts from the sidelines for so long, has finally been asked to send some ideas down onto the field for its own shot at the big time.

Your imagination, understandably, is going to get a little overly excited at its moment in the spotlight. So rather than solemnly suggesting an orderly progression of characters and story ideas, it will send an entire screaming busload of contenders careening onto the field, where they will collide with each other, knock over the marching band, and wreak unholy havoc on the turf.

This is a great, exhilarating moment, and you should ride it for all it's worth. Even if you don't know *exactly* how you're going to fit those five ninjas into your courtroom drama, hey, they've arrived. And they want to be in the book. So put them in there. Inevitably they'll do *something* for the plot. If their performance doesn't end up meriting their inclusion, you can always clip them out later.

That's the beauty of novel writing: A panoply of strange characters, spread out over cities or continents, will somehow end up banding together midbook to construct your plot. You probably won't see how this will happen early in the writing process, and you shouldn't worry about it yet. Your role as a writer in Week One is just to continue to wave all of these players down onto the field, and then write like hell to keep up with them.

With so much great input coming your way, Week One is a fantastic time to build up a comfortable word-count lead. If you're not exhausted after writing the day's 1,667-word quota, keep going to 2,000. And then to 3,000. On the first weekend of your mission, try to rack up 10,000 words if you can. You'll be *very* thankful for the cushion when you arrive at Week Two. Which is when things, ahem, change a little.

Don't Delete, *Italicize*

Even during anything-goes Week One, you'll write a few things that you recognize right away just don't fit in the book. Maybe you took a character in a new direction and didn't like it, or had a conversation that revealed too much too soon.

When you write these things, whether they constitute a sentence, a paragraph, or an entire chapter, do not cut them. All words you write on your novel, no matter how misshapen or ill-advised, still represent crucial steps toward the 50,000-word finish line.

Rather than deleting these passages, put them in italics. Italics, in its skinny, slanted way, is the next best thing to nonexistence. And your words are already flagged for evaluation when your Inner Editor returns for the rewrite phase later.

If even the sight of your italicized miscues distracts you to the point of writing inactivity, you can take things a step further and change the color of the italicized text from black to white, rendering it invisible (yet still word-countable). At the end of the month, you can use the "select all" command to turn the entire draft back to black, and go in with your editing scalpel to make your excisions.

Start a Novel Notes File

As you write, you'll come up with a number of jokes, plot developments, and bits of dialogue that would be great to slip into the book at some point in the future. While your magical noveling notebook is still the main go-to for breakthroughs and discoveries you have while out exploring the real world, you should start a Novel Notes file on your computer, and have it open at all times while writing.

Keep the Story to Yourself

This is a tough one. On the one hand, you want instant feedback from those around you to reassure yourself that you're on the right track. You also want those around you to understand what you're doing and be proud of it.

My advice, though, is to not share the novel until it's done. Feel free to read a few paragraphs aloud to loved ones, or email short

KEEPING BETH FROM BERTHA:
AVOIDING THE DREADED "NAME DRIFT"

As you christen each of your characters, be sure to jot their names down on a piece of paper that you keep close to your writing area. You'll be amazed how easily a Mike can become a Mick (who will in turn become a Matt) without some handy visual reminder to help you keep all the identities straight.

passages to friends. But even sharing a small amount of your work-in-progress will encourage you to spend some amount of time editing and revising the text so it's presentable.

This is a dangerous, slippery slope—largely because it sounds a high-pitch whistle that only your Inner Editor can hear. At which point the beast, realizing you haven't been receiving your RDA of browbeating and self-criticism lately, will begin shaking the bars of the kennel, trying to get out and come help you.

That is the kind of help you can do without.

Also, anything short of an enthusiastic ovation from your audience will likely start making you worry about the quality of your work and the direction your story has taken. Even worse, your audience might misinterpret your sharing as a request for constructive criticism. At that point, the crippling self-doubt *really* kicks in, as you've just replaced your own Inner Editor with someone else's.

As much as possible, resist the temptation to share your work-in-progress with others. After you've finished the first draft, and you've gone through and tidied up the typos and whatnot, you can show it to whoever you like and get the feedback you'll need to improve it.

Actually, come to think of it, you also should resist the temptation to share your work-in-progress with *yourself* as you write as well. Rereading parts of your novel while writing is like doubling back and rerunning portions of a marathon midrace. The best plan is to keep moving forward, allowing yourself only an orienting glimpse back into your story when you set out on each day's writing mission.

All of this advice is ignored with no ill effects every year during NaNoWriMo by hundreds of writers, who post each day's writing output on their personal Web sites. For these fearless souls, the benefits of having an audience expecting the next installment of the book outweigh the risks of critical feedback–killing momentum. It's risky, though, and if you have anything less than an unshakable sense of confidence in your book, you should be especially wary of letting too much of your book get out into the world before it's done.

WEEK ONE EXERCISES

In addition to week-specific issues and tips, we'll also highlight a couple of exercises you can do to help keep your creative juices flowing.

"Tell Me about Your Uncle": Fleshing Out Characters through Random Conversations with Friends and Strangers

As any psychologist will tell you, truth is definitely stranger than fiction. If you're having trouble coming up with interesting attributes and histories for your characters, tap into the millions of hilarious, wonderful characters already in orbit around you. Grab your notebook, call a friend, and ask them to tell you everything they know about their strangest relative.

Even some of the most mundane stories ("I had an uncle who wore flannel shirts every single day of his life. He used to sneak bologna into the zoo to throw to the gibbons because he always thought they looked too skinny.") will often spark ideas about potential characters and stories.

This tactic also works well with strangers, especially cute ones who will no doubt be impressed by this crazy novel project. So the next time you're in line at the grocery store or sitting in a coffeeshop and someone catches your eye, take out your pen and go harvest their family. You'll net a tremendous haul of anecdotes that you can steal for your story, and they'll come away telling their friends about the hot writer they met in the check-out line.

I, Couch Potato

Ah, the rigors of homework. The second exercise this week involves watching TV. Pick any show you enjoy. Just make sure it's fictional, and make sure it isn't one that you love so much that you will lose track of the assignment. Which is this: Sit down in front of the boob tube, put on your thinking cap, and watch critically.

Whatever show you've chosen, from the *Simpsons* to the *Sopranos*, keep an eye out for how the writers tackle the same challenges you're facing in your novel: trying to fit a lot of story into a little time. Most TV shows have a main plot garlanded by one or two subplots. Some give each of the show's main characters a role in processing a single plot.

How many plots does your show juggle? How long does it wait before introducing the Central Problem? How and when does it use foreshadowing to let the viewers know what's coming? How is the story divvied up between the many characters? Is the outcome predictable? If you liked some aspect of the show's story, are there structural devices—pacing, narration, anything—you can steal from it?

Dissecting a TV show is a great way to help you see the tropes of storytelling laid bare. If you're hungering for more storytelling models, pop in a DVD and watch how the same conflicts are handled in a movie. As embarrassing as it is to report—and this secret does not leave the pages of this book—I modeled the pacing of my most recent month-long novel on the animated movie *Antz* and a re-run of *Cheers*.

Sigh.

Nobel Prize Committee, here I come, right? But whatever works, works. And TV shows and movies are a treasure trove of storytelling wisdom, both good and bad.

CHAPTER  6

WEEK TWO:

Storm Clouds, Plot Flashes,

and the Return

of Reality

Dear Writer,

One week in, and we're right on target: Our homes are a mess, our friends are annoyed, and our bosses have started casting suspicious, sidelong glances at us as they walk by our cubicles.

It's been a promising beginning. In the last seven days alone, you've written a small novella's worth of people and places. And you've felt the sexy click of your imagination as it locks on target, the muscley thrill of your bad-ass creative self rolling up its sleeves and wading into the fray.

There's much to celebrate. But sadly, there's also some bad news on the way. The *No Plot? No Problem!* team of literary meteorologists have radioed an urgent message back from the noveling front. There's a storm rolling in from the west; a black howler of a tempest. And it's headed your way.

Welcome to Week Two. If you brought a poncho, now would be a good time to get it out.

The storm will likely break in three or four days, exactly at the point when the novelty of the event starts to fade, and your book starts getting more demanding.

Cue thunder. Cue lightning. And cue some big-time writerly grumpiness.

Those first thunderclaps mark an essential turning point in novel writing; it's the place where the cast has been introduced, the stage has been set, and everything is primed for the story to unfold. Having reached this stage, most novelists would pat themselves on the back and head off to Majorca for a month to celebrate their accomplishments.

But because of the pressing timeframe, you barely have time to catch your breath, much less catch a plane. For better or worse, the next great stage—plot building—is upon us.

 SO YOU WANT TO START OVER: A WARNING ABOUT DIVORCING YOUR NOVEL AND RUNNING OFF WITH A NEW STORY

Everyone, at some point, sees their novel as a lost cause. The characters are one-dimensional. The plot isn't going anywhere. The language is abysmal. For month-long novelists, this moment typically occurs in Week Two, when the general unhappiness about the hours you've been keeping and the challenges of plot improvisation make even the most promising story look like a disaster.

The thing to remember even in the darkest moments is that there *is* something great and workable in your story. Rather than starting over entirely, the best approach is usually to focus on the book's strengths— the characters or parts of the storyline you are enjoying— and let the story take off from there.

Yep. You've wrapped up the exposition, and now something book-like has to happen. Someone needs to fall in love. Or get amnesia. Or go on a road trip. But who? And how?

The questions just keep piling up, and your first impulse will likely be to chuck the whole thing and go back to the blissful life you led before this five-headed literary monster began devouring all your free time.

As you write your way through the next seven days, know that Week Two hurts so bad because you're making huge strides in your book, solving a year's worth of plot and character problems in one overcaffeinated week.

The answers will come. Just keep at it, and before you know it, Week Two will be a distant memory. The sun will be shining again, the way will be clear, and the writing will become fun once more.

And Week Three! Oh, don't get me started about the wonders of Week Three. There are some amazing things on your literary horizons. The kinds of breakthroughs that will make you laugh and cry and shake your head pityingly at friends and family members who wasted this month on empty pursuits like conversation, bathing, and sleep.

The only way to get to that self-righteously pitying stage, though, is by hurling yourself directly into the eye of Week Two's storms. Now is the time to batten down the hatches and throw yourself into your story with everything you've got.

You've made such great progress, writer. And the best is just around the bend.

WEEK TWO ISSUES

Still No Plot? Still No Problem.

If you already know the intricacies of how your novel is going to unfold, Week Two is the point when you'll begin putting your fiendish plan into action. The players are in position, and it's time to tip that first domino, to open the story's throttle and watch it speed ahead.

If you still don't know what your characters are doing in your book, Week Two is the point when you should panic.

Hee hee.

Just kidding.

Having a shaky, hazy, or problematic plot heading into Week Two is absolutely fine, and is a predicament common to many month-long novelists. I guarantee that if you meet your word count quota over the next seven days, you'll have a much, much clearer idea of what your book is about by the end of the week.

As I said before, plot is just the movement of your characters through time, over the course of your book. If you're still not clear on your book's plot, the best thing you can do for your story is to really let your characters *move* this week. Give them space to show parts of themselves they may have kept hidden in the first seven days. Encourage them to act out, to indulge their desires, no matter how zany or destructive those desires may be. Allow change, and plot will happen.

Character Coups

If you're have trouble seeing a possible plot in your novel, one of the problems may be your growing boredom or disenchantment with your main characters. If you've been noticing that, despite your best intentions, the camera lens of your book tends to drift to the incidental members of the cast—the best friend, the co-worker, or the family iguana, say—it may be a sign that the book would be better re centered in their orbit.

Demoting your hero from savior to sidekick and promoting some of your supporting characters to starring roles happens a lot in the figuring-it-out-as-you-go world of month-long novel-writing. Before you do anything drastic, sit down and think about story directions and exciting imbroglios that might spin-off from your new potential protagonist(s). If you come up with a few good ones, or find yourself salivating at the thought of letting someone else take the spotlight from the dullard currently narrating your story, a character coup may be for you.

Falling Behind and the Key to the VIP Lounge

Okay, let's be honest: There will be days in this wild escapade when you're just not feeling it. When your brain has checked out and

 ## AXE-MURDERERS AND SELF-DECEPTION: AVOIDING THE DEMON PLAGUE OF SELF-EDITING

"The best trick I've learned is to lie to myself. When, in chapter seven, I write something that contradicts something written earlier, I tell myself that I already made the necessary corrections in chapter three. I just tell myself that the earlier parts are the way I need them to be for me to write something that day which builds on them."
—Russell Kremer, 51, three-time NaNoWriMo winner from Los Angeles

"Imagine the pages you have written to be an axe-wielding maniac, hellbent on massacring your creative flow. Get away from those pages as quickly as possible. Don't worry how awkwardly or clumsily you do so. The very life of your book is at stake. As soon as you look back over previous pages, the doom will be upon you."
—Trena Taylor, 34, two-time NaNoWriMo winner from London

"I write parts of my novels as emails. I simply open up Outlook or Yahoo! or whatever, address it to myself, and just start writing. Something about the rhetorical situation of email writing keeps my internal censor and editor quiet (or quieter at least)."
—Ed Chang, 33, three-time NaNoWriMo winner from Washington, D.C.

neglected to leave a forwarding address, and it's all you can do to get the food from the dinner plate to your mouth before you collapse, asleep, at the table.

These days will come more often than you might like in Week Two, and to avoid getting overwhelmed, now is a great time to give yourself the occasional novel-free night. Even if you're behind on your word count, taking a night off to replenish those overtaxed synapses will likely end up boosting your productivity in the long run.

Whenever you do skip a writing day, though, be sure to make up the words within a couple of days. As you know all too well by now, every day you skip steers you another 1,667 words off course. Accumulate three or four wordless days in a row, and the book becomes less of a spontaneous creative experiment and more of a ten-round grudge match between you and your hulking literary deficit.

Staying on pace, on the other hand, grants you access to the *No Plot? No Problem!* VIP Writer's Lounge. This swank place is the finest writer's nook in the world; the coffee is free, the people are friendly and inspiring, and the chairs are all orthopedic custom jobbies with expansive lumbar support.

The VIP Lounge is an ideal refuge from some of the rough weather that will be passing over your novel in Week Two. Do what you can to haul yourself up into its ritzy confines, but remember that *staying reasonably sane is the week's ultimate goal.* If you have to take on some word debt to keep burnout at bay, do so. You can always set up residency in the VIP Lounge next week.

WEEK TWO TIPS

"Don't Get It Right, Get It Written": Making Decisions in Week Two

When asked for the most important piece of first-draft writing insight she's ever received, Edgar Award–winning mystery writer

Julie Smith quoted some advice from her newspaper days. "Don't get it right, Smith," a gruff editor had told her. "Get it written."

That advice looms large over Week Two, and it is something to keep in mind as you decide what to do with all these characters that have taken up residency in your book.

The variety of directions a book can take are a little daunting. Do you kill someone off? Burn down a house? Fling a character into space via intergalactic wormhole?

In deciding what should happen next in your book, know that all plot points lead to the same happy place: getting a complete draft of your novel done. You aren't shooting for perfection here; you're just exploring the outer reaches of your imagination, and building a book one day at a time. Don't worry about getting it right this week. That will come in the revisions. This week, your goal is just to get it written.

 OBSESSIVE COUNTING DISORDER

Psychologists have a term for people who perform small gestures and rituals over and over again uncontrollably: obsessive-compulsive disorder. Month-long novelists who don't already have OCD will be getting a crash course in the mental illness thanks to the "word count" feature built into most word processors. Nothing is more alluring than pulling up a tally of your progress as you type, and you'll likely find yourself checking your word count after every paragraph. Assessing your progress after every couple of lines, though, is like checking the odometer every five minutes on a thousand-mile road trip—knowing how far you've gone does nothing to get you there faster, and it makes the journey seem interminably slow. One way to get around this is to structure your writing around units of time rather than numbers of words, and then make word counting a reward you earn at the end of each noveling session.

CHEAP PADDING TECHNIQUES: EASY TRICKS FOR GETTING YOUR WORD COUNT UP WHEN YOU'RE FEELING DOWN

There will be times in your writing journey when you want to crawl under the nearest boulder, curl up, and die. These moments will pass, but desperate times call for desperate measures, and there are a host of word-count-increasing tricks that well-seasoned month-long novelists use to help pad their novels (and warm their spirits) in these dark hours.

Here are some of the old standbys:

The stutter: Afflict one of your characters with a stutter, and it doubles the girth of their dialogue, and it also allows the supporting cast to spend several pages wondering in great, word-count bolstering detail about the sudden, mysterious onset of the speech impediment.

Temporary deafness: Everything from loud rock concerts to small deposits of earwax can temporarily render your character deaf, necessitating that everything said to him or her be repeated. And repeated. And repeated.

The dream sequence: Our dreams might as well come with a sign that says, "Free words: Help yourself." The dream sequence (and its cousin, the hallucination) go on for as long as you like and don't have to make any sense whatsoever. It's the motherlode!

The citation: If your character can read, you can cite. Give your protagonist a copy of *Beowulf* and an annoying habit of reading poetry out loud on their long commute to work, and you've suddenly added thousands of words to your count. This also works with songs, newspaper articles, and—gulp—other novels.

The extended name: Okay, say your protagonist is named Jane. Every occurrence of Jane's name only nets you a single tick on the word counter. Now let's say you use the find-and-replace function on your word processor to change "Jane" to "Jane Marie." Presto! You've doubled your investment. This works especially well in fantasy novels, where a low-yield name like Hrudon can, with a single find-and-replace search, become "Hrudon, Son of Sankar, Prince and Overlord of Outer Cthandon."

De-hyphenate: Word-processing programs tend to count hyphenated words as a single unit. "Lilly-livered" is just one word; "not-quite-as-potent-as-promised fungicide" counts as only two words. Deleting your hyphens may lose you grammar points, but it will definitely gain you words when you're too tired to write any new ones.

The Mind Is Willing, the Immune System Weak: Avoiding Pathogens and Other Enemies of Fine Literature

Colds, flus, and other opportunistic viruses are the failed writers of the microbe world. They have a good story to tell, but they lack the drive, discipline, and typing appendages to get the stories down on paper. Like most stymied creative types, they'll stop at nothing to bring down the brave few who dare to seize their dreams.

Because of this, you should guard your health very, very carefully from this point forward. Especially if you've been sleeping four hours a night and eating most of your meals at Taco Bell.

Wash your hands with soap every time you pass a faucet. Eat as many fruits and vegetables as you can stomach. Start stirring vitamin C into your coffee or whiskey shots. And if you are in a public space—such as a restaurant or an airplane cabin—and someone begins coughing, flee immediately. Your body will thank you, and your novel will thank you, too.

The Check-In: Staying in Touch When You Don't Have Time to Write

On days when you don't have the time or energy for a full writing session, you can help keep your word debt low with quick writing sessions I call Check-Ins. These are noveling quickies where you just poke your head into your novel for twenty minutes or so, add a pinch of color here, an embellishment there, and then call it a night after 500 words or so.

It may seem like a pitiful drop in the bucket, but every word you write is one less you'll have to tackle the next day. The main point of a Check-In, though, is to help you maintain a creative connection to your book so your imagination will continue to nibble away at the story until you sit down for the next full blown write-in.

USING EMAIL TO MAKE FREE BACKUPS OF YOUR NOVEL

Computers, unfortunately, go belly-up all the time. Protect yourself from being one of the sad, sad novelists who lose their best work when their operating system dissolves by making frequent backups of your novel. The best way to do this is simply to email your novel to yourself as an attachment every few days, leaving the email unopened on the server until the next backup arrives. Hopefully you'll never need to access the novel attachment, but just in case you do, it's there.

WEEK TWO EXERCISES

Getting On Your Case:
How Friends and Family Can Help Plot Your Novel

In the business school world, the teaching of proper management is partly done through nifty things called business cases. These are swashbuckling tales of the exploits of managers and employees at companies where change (or the lack thereof) is threatening the well-being of the organization. Business cases lead students through the who and where of the story right up to the point when a strategic decision needs to be made to decide the fate of the company. And then the MBA students must debate what they'd do if they were in the CEO's or middle manager's shoes.

The same teaching aid that's transformed mild-mannered graduate students into ruthless, bloodthirsty entrepreneurs can also be harnessed to help you gain new insights on your book. This week, try making a business case out of your novel.

Here's how it works: Ask a couple of friends who enjoy the same kinds of books you do to meet with you for an hour (you can heighten the Fortune 500 mood by dressing in corporate duds and bringing your notes in a briefcase). Then, once everyone's comfortable, hand out some scratch paper and pens, and explain the ground rules: You are going to give them a handful of characters, a setting, and a *veeery* vague story direction, and they are to tell you what should happen next.

Explain everything you know about your characters, one by one—where they work, who they love, what they're embarrassed by, and so on. Encourage your story students to jot down questions and ideas as they occur to them, but be sure to emphasize that this is a brainstorming session, not a test; there are no right or wrong story directions.

After you've completely described all of your characters and their connections to each other, your job is to get the conversational ball rolling and then become invisible. Let your audience argue, debate, and build off one another's ideas as you take notes on everything they say. Even if you already know what will happen in your book, you'll get amazing insights on motivations, subplots, and other nefarious activities that might make your book more interesting.

When your focus group inevitably asks what *you* think should happen in the story, be sure to keep your ideas a mystery. As mentioned in chapter five, revealing your book's plot before it's written can end up sapping a lot of the joy from the writing process, especially if your focus group has a tepid reaction to it—or thinks it stinks. Just keep scribbling down notes and ideas, and let them know that all will be revealed when the book comes out in hardback.

Inciting Plot Flashes

No one has better encapsulated the spirit of month-long noveling than three-time NaNoWriMo winner Rise Sheridan-Peters, who describes her approach to writing as follows: "I don't wait for my muse to wander by; I go out and drag her home by the hair."

With time being of the essence this month, any hairy handhold you can use to hurry your novel along should be exploited. And certain activities work much better than others to stimulate the copious "aha!" breakthrough moments you'll have during your noveling month. I call these moments "plot flashes," and inconveniently, most of them occur while you're faraway from a keyboard.

For me, common sites for plot flashes include hot showers, dance clubs, and long bike rides. For some reason, creative juices just percolate better when accompanied by routine, automatic motions. When I set out on my bike for a five-mile ride, I *know* that I'll come home with invaluable material I didn't have before. Which is also why I take a notebook and pen out every time I go dancing.

Other NaNoWriMo winners recommend crapping, walking a dog, jumping on a bed, and flitting around at the edge of sleep as possible doorways to plot flashes. Try all of these and more this week, and see if any help you unleash your imagination.

CHAPTER 7

WEEK THREE:
Clearing Skies, Warmer
Weather, and a
Jetpack on Your Back

Dear Writer,

Welcome to Week Three! If last week was a stormy trek through ice-slicked mountain passes, Week Three is ... well ... nicer. *Much* nicer.

You've survived the most difficult part of the month. You still have a lot of work ahead, but the weather is more forgiving in Week Three, and the landscape softer. In the amiable confines of Week Three, gentle woodland creatures will begin appearing along the trail's edge, chanting your name, extending trays of nutrient-rich acorns and hollowed gourds brimming with Gatorade.

Or at least let's hope it's Gatorade.

Anyway, you should drink it all in. For this is the week when you begin to head downhill, when the beautiful, bucolic patch of earth called The End first becomes visible.

To get the most out of Week Three, there are two things you must do:

1) Lose any word debt you've accumulated.

If you fell behind in the grim slog of Week Two, you'll need to turn the productivity up a notch or three. To help enable this, the *No Plot? No Problem!* Employment Outreach Team has talked to your boss and brokered an agreement: You are henceforth allowed to novel on company time as long as nobody sees you doing it. (Under the terms of this agreement, you are also allowed to print out three copies of your finished novel on the office laser printer after everyone's gone home for the night.)

Whether you're writing from home or work, the month's timetable says you should have about 35,000 words by the end of this week. Ignore this timetable if you're far behind, focusing instead on hitting 30,000 words by the week's close. Whatever you do, though, breach the 30s by the dawn of Week Four.

2) Let gravity be your guide.

Things open up toward the middle of Week Three. The pitch of the noveling trail will shift beneath your feet, pointing you downhill at a steep slope. As your tale picks up speed, your first reaction may

 CAN I GIVE UP NOW?

No. You cannot give up now.

be to try to slow yourself, to steady your progress to an even and orderly pace.

Screw that. This is your time to fly.

Why? Because it's all going to start coming together this week. The ninjas your imagination randomly introduced in your courtroom drama back in Week One? They'll appear before the judge this week with some testimony that will turn the case *upside down*. The unstoppable zombies terrorizing the Phish concert will cease their marauding and begin to stagger as a single, piercing guitar note rings out over the crowd. And lowly bartender Ngiam Ton Boon at the Raffles Hotel in Singapore will reach out for gin and grab cherry brandy by mistake, changing the destiny of colonial-era alcoholics forever.

Week Three is when it all happens—when all those loose ends begin lashing themselves together as if by magic, creating connections and passageways through your novel that are both apt and effortless. Do well in this week, and the novel is yours for the taking.

WEEK THREE ISSUES

Standing Halfway and Seeing the Future: Appraising Your Progress

You've officially crossed the continental divide of your novel month at this point. Congratulations! Now is a perfect moment for you to put word count issues aside, size up your story, and figure out how close you are to The End.

In your guesstimation, are you:

A) More than halfway through with your story?

B) Exactly halfway through with your story?

C) Less than halfway through with your story?

If you answered A or B, hallelujah. Great job. Continue full speed ahead. You're right on track with the pacing. If you're worried about running out of story before you hit 50,000 words, don't. For one, you probably have more wrapping up to do than you realize. And for two, a prologue, epilogue, and table of contents can always be conjured at the last minute to push your book over the edge of 50,000 words. There will be plenty for you to do if you reach the end of your novel before you reach the summit of your word count, so write quickly and with confidence.

If you answered C, though, we need to talk.

The goal here is to have your 49,999th and 50,000th words be "The" and "End." Not because your book will really be 50,000 words when you've had a chance to edit it. In fact, your story will probably gain an extra 10,000 to 50,000 words around its midsection during revisions.

No, you should try to write a complete story this month because you'll find the visionary work of creation becomes much, much more difficult after your #A30/31/50k deadline expires and your Inner Editor moves back home to live with you again.

For the next two weeks of writing, you will be bathing in dizzying amounts of momentum and literary moxie. You'll be closer to your characters than you may ever be again. All of which makes this the perfect time to nail down major decisions regarding plot and storyline.

If you are still introducing characters and haven't yet sent them out in search of a plot, you should sit down and figure out where they're going *now*. What are the essential scenes you can focus on writing over the next two weeks so that you can have an entire story arc completed in two weeks' time? Skip ahead if you need to—using lots of in-text notes ("here is where the podiatrist will admit to Nancy that he's an alien") to keep track of the parts you're skipping over—and write only those scenes that move the story forward.

It can be disheartening to realize that you aren't going to be able to write every scene in your novel before the month ends, but I can tell you from experience that it is *much* easier to fill in connecting scenes and interludes during rewriting than it is to have to conceive and write the final five chapters of a story after the month has ended. Avoid that by bending your story arc now so its tail-end is pointing squarely at 50k.

"You're Still Working on that Thing?": When Support Networks Attack

Some NaNoWriMo participants are blessed with fanatical cheering sections and relentlessly supportive groups of friends and family who constantly ply them for details about their work-in-progress. These good-hearted folks make care packages stuffed with frozen pizzas and unmarked bills, and listen, enraptured, to the stories about life as an amateur novelist.

The other 99 percent of us have a somewhat less saintly support network. Our caregivers are dispensing bemused glances on good days, and are hurling our unwashed dishes at our heads on bad ones.

However, no matter how enthusiastic or disinterested your fans have been up till now, you'll probably notice an ebbing in their support this week.

It makes sense. Having a novel appear in your life so suddenly is like finding a baby—or a very small person convincingly dressed as a baby—on your doorstep. As you acclimate to the new presence in your life, old routines go out the window, and friends and family are inevitably pushed aside as you figure out how best to make room for the addition.

And like a baby, a novel is largely a personal miracle; the tiny joys of your writing process usually won't resonate with other people, no matter how close you are to them.

Like many month-long writers, three-time winner Rise Sheridan-Peters finds this discrepancy between the joy of the book and the sorrow of friends and family especially pernicious in Week Three.

"I'm finally figuring out what the book is about," Rise says, "and everyone else in my life is counting the days until the book is done. I want them to sit and look at me raptly while I tell them that what's inside the suitcase turned out to be a forged reliquary with a fake saint's arm that's actually filled with designer drugs from a lab at MIT. They just want to know if we're ever going to eat another meal that didn't come in a bag with a plastic spork."

As you head into your third week of missed social engagements and poor performance on household chores, your friends and loved ones will be slowly realizing that if you were going to quit your book, you probably would have done so already. Which means another two weeks of closed doors and sporky dinners.

This may bring out a little grouchiness in your support team, mostly because they miss you. Or they at least miss the less annoying version of you who could sit through an entire movie without later discussing how many words you could have written in that two-hour period.

So, give a little love and understanding back, and assure your support networks that the thing is almost over.

WEEK THREE TIPS

Activating the 6,000-Word Jetpack Under Your Seat

Tremendous come-from-behind victories have been a part of month-long noveling since the dawn of the sport. One of the easiest ways to go from out-of-contention to head-of-the-pack is by harnessing the power of 6,000-word days. These are much easier to pull off than you might imagine.

Here is a step-by-step guide to turning on your noveling jetpack:

1) Pick a Saturday or Sunday when you have approximately two-hour pockets of free time spread throughout the morning, afternoon, and evening.

WHAT DO I DO IF I HIT 50,000 WORDS EARLY?

Every year, about 2 percent of National Novel Writing Month participants have that rare combination of fleet-fingered typing skills and well-oiled imaginations that allow them to hit 50,000 words after a couple of weeks. If you find yourself among this golden group and cross the 50,000-word threshold in Week Three, then write like the wind until you reach the end of the story. If you've typed "The End" and still have a couple of days (and some energy) remaining, dive back into the middle sections of your book and begin fleshing out and realigning text to fit with whatever changes in story direction you've enacted over the course of the novel. In other words, just keep going, superstar!

2) Wake up early and have a large, healthy breakfast. Or some coffee and a cigarette, whichever is easiest.

3) Do three 30-minute writing sessions in a row, separated by 10-minute stretching/wrist-shaking/fetal-position-holding and complaining breaks.

4) Go have fun, and come back and repeat the same 3/30/10 schedule feat after lunch.

5) Do something else, and after dinner and some post-meal loafing, head to the computer and do another three 30-minute sessions.

6) At this point, you will have added 6,000 words to your tally, and can go to sleep dreaming of friendly agents bringing oversized advance checks to your door.

To exponentially increase the power of your jetpack, follow this regimen two days in a row. You will be floored by how much more lovable the world is when you add 12,000 words to your count over one weekend.

Out of Sight But Not Out of Mind:
Banishing the Last Traces of Your Inner Editor

News from your Inner Editor! I just dropped by the kennel, and your Inner Editor is doing *very* well in your absence. While I was there, it was in the middle of correcting the pitch and pronunciation of a group of elementary-school carolers who had come by to spread good cheer.

I've never seen an editor so happy.

Despite your IE's contented distance, you may still be feeling its presence this week in the form of writing or creative blocks. If you are feeling stymied at Week Three, you were probably cursed with a more dictatorial Inner Editor than most. Here are some ways for you to cope with this style-cramping, book-blocking situation.

1) Break things.

Don't break real-world things (which tend to be expensive), but things in your novel. Your Inner Editor has long served the role of an overly protective parent. Now that your parent is out of town, it's time you leveraged those lessons from *Risky Business, Sixteen Candles,* and other helpful high school instructional videos: It's time to throw a party and trash the house.

Pick out a character that's been causing you no end of grief, and do something big and reckless with them. Have them exiled out of the story or get swallowed by a wormhole while waiting for the bus. If you've hit a standstill in your efforts to bring two obviously perfect romantic leads together, kill one of them. Your readers won't see it coming, and in figuring out how to fix the mess you've just made of your story, you'll give your imagination the kind of fertile improvisational environment it needs to thrive.

USING YOUR REFERENCE NOVEL FOR QUICK-AND-EASY PLOT VOODOO

Sometimes plot decisions require a helping hand. In these cases, I've found my reference novel (one of the essential writerly tools described in chapter three) doubles as an invaluable fortune-telling device to help guide the masterpiece-in-progress. It works like this:

You: (picking up the reference novel) Oh, Great Reference Novel! I have a question!

Book: (...)

You: My main character has the personality of a wood chip. Should I kill her off now, and re-center the story on the time-traveling family of chipmunks living under her front porch?

You: (flipping through the pages of the book, stopping on a random page, and reading the first complete sentence on the page)

Book: The accordion proved to be Angeline's favorite instrument, much to her parents' dismay.

You: Thank you, great book. She will die at noon.

---

2) Make a pact with yourself to eventually destroy all evidence that this novel ever existed.

Part of your blockage may be the fact that you're already worrying about what people are going to say about your rough draft. This is an unnecessary worry, as everyone's month-long novels are crappy, but you can address the worry directly by figuring out how you'll destroy your novel as soon as it's finished. Will you print it out, then burn it on the barbecue grill? Or bury the thing in the woods by the light of a full moon?

Once you absolutely remove from your mind the possibility that anyone else will read your work, you'll likely find yourself enjoying the writing process much more. Also, destroying your novel before anyone reads it will give you a sexy allure that's part Zen letting-go and part Jimi Hendrix writhing over his flaming Telecaster. Yeeeowch.

3) Go small.

If you've stopped writing because you can't shake the feeling that all of your plot directions are unworthy, give your plotting brain a break by focusing on things that *won't* advance the story. Write 2,000 words about a sign dangling from a hot dog stand across the street from your protagonist's house. Spend pages describing the perfume your love interest wears, and why it's exactly the wrong thing for her. Write around the periphery of your story. Write beside or below your story. But whatever you do, just keep writing. Even if you spend the next couple of days writing background material, you'll have built a hell of a great nest for your story when you find your groove again.

WEEK THREE EXERCISES

Putting Your Story on the Map

One of the worst things about being an adult is not getting to color as often as we should. This week, give your monitor-burned eyeballs a rest for an hour or so and go old-school, forsaking the computer for a big piece of blank paper and some colored pencils or crayons.

The goal of this exercise is to make a map of your fictional world. On the map, you should include all of your characters' homes, their schools or workplaces, and any places they've already visited in the book. This may be the first time that you've thought about the spatial layout of your world, so feel free to make things up as you go.

After you've placed everything that already exists in your book on the map, go in with a loose hand and start creatively filling in and adding other details and landmarks, everything from beaches to parks to clocktowers to cathedrals to bondage-gear shops. It's okay to get a little crazy, adding an ancient amphitheater behind a dry cleaning shop, or a whale-harpooning station atop City Hall. The map is partially for referencing later, but it's also a creative exercise

THOUGHTS FROM THE TRENCHES: NANOWRIMO WINNERS ON THE MIDDLE OF THE JOURNEY

"The middle bit is both good and bad, depending on how much pre-planning you've done. If you've used up all your planned events, you're screwed as you try to find new things for the characters to do. If you've never had a plan for them at all, you're screwed as you've got to start thinking about why they're actually there and what they've got to pull off by the end."
—Andrew Johnson, 29, three-time NaNoWriMo winner from Christchurch, New Zealand

"It's tough. You're either in a groove, you're procrastinating, or you're feeling really overwhelmed. Usually a bit of all three. By Week Three, panic starts to set in as you scramble to catch up if you're behind. But you've got a solid count and if it's your first time, this is probably more than you've ever written before in your life on one story. It's a terrific ego boost."
—Stacy Katz, 30, one-time NaNoWriMo winner from Houston

"The hardest thing to deal with mid-month is the disbelief of friends. 'Are you still writing that? You were *serious*? Come on, we'll just go have a quick pint...' And the growing desire to succumb to every diversion known to man. Even doing dishes. Even staying late at the office to do actual work. Anything to put off having to face those thousands of unwritten words."
—Trena Taylor, 34, two-time NaNoWriMo winner from London

in its own right. It's a chance to draw up your world just for fun and to see if any of these off-the-cuff imaginings might be something you'd like to incorporate into your noveling reality.

Also, don't feel constrained to drawing just one kind of map. For dramas that unfold mostly indoors, you may want to create a floor-by-floor schematic drawing of the important homes, shops, or restaurants, rather than mapping your book on a street-by-street level. Topographic maps may be helpful if you're writing a story that relies on encampments or precipitous shifts in altitude.

Finally, make sure to color everything in as vividly as possible. Since this exercise is a great way to procrastinate from writing your book, take as long as you like perfecting the algae slick on the town pond with a realistic shade of green.

When you're done, keep the map close at hand as an update-able inspiration-generator and a handy reminder of where things are in your book.

The Person & Thing Game

For those looking to spice up their writing with some random (and word-count bolstering) creativity, this exercise is a time-tested winner.

To play it, you'll need a public space and an unread newspaper. You'll also need a pen and your notebook. This works best as a two-player game, but it can also be fun as a solo challenge.

Here's how the game works: Sit in a public space with plenty of foot traffic. Close your eyes, and count to fifteen. When you open your eyes, the first person you see is your Person. Write down everything about them you can before they get away—their clothes, their carriage, their race, their hairstyle, what they're holding; anything and everything.

Next, take your newspaper, and close your eyes again. Open your newspaper to a random page and, keeping your eyes closed, run your finger over the page, stopping after a couple of seconds.

The article, advertisement, or photo you're pointing to has a deep connection to the Person you just collected. What's the connection? You have to figure it out, and you have to work that person and their issue convincingly into the next chapter of your novel.

The more people you collect and successfully incorporate into each chapter, the more points you get in the game. If you're playing with someone else, you alternate collecting people and their issues; each person harvests his or her own random characters and looks up their backstories in the newspaper. Then both of you set off to write, coming back together at the end of the noveling period to read each other the passages featuring your random cameos.

Extended game: You can add an atlas and play the Person, Place & Thing Game. With eyes closed, randomly flip open to a page to add a country or state of origin for your collected person.

CHAPTER **8**

WEEK FOUR:
Champagne
>   and the Roar
of the Crowd

Dear Writer,

This is where it all comes together. Week Four. The sink or swim, do or die, zero hour. Or hours. You have 168 of them left. Assuming you sleep eight hours a night, and are otherwise occupied twelve hours per day, that's 16 hours—or 1,680 plump, succulent word-filled writing minutes—ahead of you.

But before we delve too deeply into the math of your imminent triumph, I need you to do me a favor. I'd like you to put this book down, put on your shoes, grab your keys, and go to the grocery store.

Seriously.

Go now.

Okay, go later. Whenever it's convenient. But make sure, when you're at the store, to pick up two bottles of champagne. If you are underage, you can pick up a champagne substitute, such as beer.

Then bring the two bottles home and hide both away at the back of the fridge. We'll be needing them later.

Now, back to life in your novel.

It's Week Four. You're so close to the end of the month you can taste it. And whether you're at 14,000 or 40,000 words, there's probably a part of you that's asking: Haven't I written enough already? Do I *really* need to go any further? Why don't I just bow out now, and wrap up the manuscript in a couple of months, when I'm less tired and have a better supply of clean underwear?

These are all good questions.

And here's the answer: The next seven days will pass in the blink of an eye. To be replaced by another seven. And another seven after that.

Before you know it, the weeks will become months, which will fast become years. In no time, you'll be eighty-five years old and sitting

THE (COLD) WINDS OF CHANGE: PUTTING WEATHER IN YOUR STORY

"Nothing breaks up an author's progress like having to stop every few pages to fuss-up the weather." —Mark Twain

Weather is one of those things you don't really think about while you're reading a novel. Unlike the weather in real life, novel weather is mostly a low-key affair. Either it's cold or hot, rainy or not. If you find yourself winding your story down before you hit 50,000 words, consider spending some time adding exquisite weather to your book. Describe the warm winds and put smells in the air. Send in a monsoon, and follow a raindrop in its broken progress from cloud to gutter. Weather, as boring as it sounds, can actually be amazingly fun to write.

on a porch somewhere, looking back on your life, and reminiscing about all the many things you've accomplished.

And when you get to that point, I promise you this: Those activities and errands that seem so essential right now—composing the company's annual report, passing that English exam, arranging for competent child care—all of these things that seem so crucial will not be recalled with pride or fondness.

In fact, you won't remember a single one of them.

Decades from now, however, you *will* remember that ineffable moment when the word counter ran it's computery calculation over your book and announced you had reached the 50,000-word endpoint. You'll smilingly recall that time you were stupid enough to sign up for the challenge of a lifetime, and mighty enough to see it through. You will remember that month, that hectic, harried month, when you made a promise to yourself, when you set off on an impossible quixotic quest, and *nailed* it.

Do you see where I'm going with this?

You are on the verge of pulling off something incredible here. You have many more words to write and, given the short time remaining, success may involve hard work. But over these past three weeks you've honed all the skills you need to pull this off—to glide over that finish line.

You *can* do this. Just make the time to write, however much time it takes. Move forward, relentless, determined, confident.

And as you cross these last few miles, savor them. For the pain is almost over, and the celebrations are about to begin.

WEEK FOUR ISSUES

Arriving at 35,000 Words

The only thing remotely close to the emotional elation of hitting 50,000 words is reaching 35,000 words. Everything eases up at 35,000.

HOW TO MAKE YOUR PRINTOUT LOOK MORE LIKE A REAL BOOK

For a truly polished presentation, number your pages and your chapters, and insert a page break after the end of each one. (To do this go to Insert on your word-processing document, and choose Break, then Page Break.) Now change the document layout to the Landscape setting, and then divide each page into two very wide columns with a two-inch gutter between them. Voila! Bookish, indeed.

This is the penultimate lap; the on-ramp to the 40s; the place where the chunk of work separating you from "The End" can be whittled down to nothing in a matter of days. Thirty-five thousand words is where you get your third wind, and the writing from here on out will remind you of those breezy, blissful days of Week One.

Holiday Horror Stories:
Surviving Family Vacations with Your Word Count Intact

If you are writing your book during November or, God help you, December, you'll have the wildcard of the holidays thrown into your final writing sessions. Though these often mean time off work or school, they also bring a host of family obligations. Surviving Thanksgiving or Christmas with your word count intact takes some finessing, especially if it involves long drives and airport layovers.

If you are going to be ending your month with your family, the most important step is to let them know ahead of time that you'll be bringing a time-sucking project home with you. Explaining to your relatives that you'll be physically present for the holidays but not entirely mentally there can be accomplished tactfully by (re)using some of the "I'm writing a novel" talking points from chapter two.

Another time-tested holiday tip for endgame novelists is to rent a motel room instead of staying at a relative's house. This way, you'll always have a quiet, controlled writing retreat when you need it. If a motel is out of the question, or if you are hosting the holidays at your place, figure out in advance what room (or, more likely, what spidery corner of the basement) might be designated a semi-private "writing area."

Three-time winner Erin Allday and her sister, Liana, found an extra bedroom served as a usable-if-imperfect writing station when their family came for a Thanksgiving visit one year.

"For four days, my parents and grandmother were staying with us in our two-bedroom apartment," Erin remembers. "My sister and I shared a bed and a computer for those four days. We regularly fought over who got to lock herself in the bedroom and write while the other one cooked and entertained.

"My parents, meanwhile, were not at all understanding about the importance of finishing our novels. We kept trying to explain why we had to retreat to the bedroom to write, but I think they assumed we were just trying to get away from all of the family."

If you know that working on your novel over the holiday is going to cause a family uprising, the best approach may be to lie. Explain that you are doing a family history project that requires you to shut yourself away from the family for most of the holiday so you can better recollect some of the memorable things grandma has said at the dinner table over the years.

Crossing the Finish Line

Yep. It's going to happen this week. I tend to celebrate crossing over with a meditative ceremony where I print the book out and neatly stack its pages on the floor. When everything has been properly laid out, I take a few steps back from the work, close my eyes, and offer up my thanks to the writing powers for another bountiful harvest. At which point, I get a running start and dive headlong into my wordpile, rolling around and snorting like a pig.

And then I fall asleep for three days.

How you celebrate is up to you. But know you can't possibly overdo the whooping, hollering, and carrying on. No matter what your neighbors might say.

WEEK FOUR TIPS

Love Your Body

After three weeks of high-intensity typing, even the most robust bodies are feeling some pain. From your wrists to your hands to your back and neck, the human body wasn't made to do the kind of gloriously sustained creative work that you've spent the last three weeks putting it through. Throughout this final week, you should pay special attention to your body's needs, and take breaks every fifteen minutes to stretch the muscles in your shoulders and arms. During Week Four, your eyes will also take on the feel of desiccated cashews. Don't rub them: What they need is for you to stop staring so intently at your monitor for hours on end. Make a point of looking back and forth, from the far distance to the near distance every five minutes or so. Also, eyedrops. Keep buckets of medicated solution on hand to douse your eyeballs at the first sign of dryness.

Troll Your Novel Notes File for Forgotten Ideas

In the manic pace of the last week, you may completely forget that genius plot turn you came up with in the previous weeks. As Week Four begins, look through both your noveling notebook and your computer novel notes file to make sure you get in all the good stuff before the curtain closes on the month.

Cross Early and Keep Writing

As I've mentioned, you are currently enveloped by a special bad-ass writing energy that will dissipate when the four weeks expire. If you still have a couple of days left to go in the month after you cross the 50k finish line, try to get back in the writing saddle after your celebration and keep going. Everything you can do now will pay off huge dividends later. Plus, building up a wordy surplus before the month draws to a close means you can go back and delete all those abysmal italicized passages *and* still have a 50,000-word novel to show your friends at the month's close.

When It Happens, Tell Everyone You Know

It's clear that the satisfaction of having written a book in a month is its own reward for this crazy endeavor. A better reward, however, is bragging to all your friends and loved ones about your enormous accomplishment. And the best way to maximize your boasting potential is by sending out an email with a "screen shot" of your winning word count total as an attachment.

Here's how you do it on a PC:

1) Take your novel to a page that you won't mind your family and friends reading (the title page is a classy option).

2) Go up and select Word Count for the entire novel, and make sure the square word count box displaying the total is visible in the middle of the screen.

3) Find the Print Screen button on your computer. Note: It may be deviously labeled "Prt Scrn." When you hit the button, it will take a picture of whatever is on your screen at the time.

4) Go to the Windows Start bar, then Programs, then Accessories, and open the cheap-o default paint program that came with your computer (it will probably be called Paint).

5) Go up to the Edit drop-down menu and select the Paste option.

6) You should now see the photo of your word-processing screen that your computer took a few seconds earlier.

7) Save the file somewhere on your desktop, and then email it to every single person you've ever met in your whole life.

Mac users activate their screen capture by hitting the command, shift, and "3" keys simultaneously. This will save a file (probably called "Photo One") to your startup disk, which can then be opened and cropped in a paint or design program.

WEEK FOUR EXERCISES

Doing the Last Days Longhand: Your Novel, Unplugged

If you're far behind schedule, ignore this exercise completely and continue your typing frenzy. If you've managed to build up a word cushion, though, consider unplugging yourself from your computer this week and walking across the finish line *au naturel.*

That's right, I'm talking about the lost art of longhand noveling. By writing part of your book with pen and paper, you'll be forced to take your story slower (something you probably haven't been doing much of this month), giving you the chance to reflect a little before committing words to the page. And from the scrabbling sound of pen on page to the spiky divot of the nib digging into the fresh expanses of paper, there's also something sensual and calming about writing by hand. If there's something we *all* could use a little more of in Week Four, it's calm.

For advice on taking a longhand vacation, I asked one-time winner Jennifer McCreedy, one of only a half dozen or so NaNoWriMo participants to have written their 50,000-word novels entirely by hand, to give us her top five tips:

1) Buy a notebook with lined paper that does not have perforated sheets. Opt for notebooks with a more durable binding than your average glue, such as stenos, which generally have sewn bindings.

2) Ditch the Wite-Out. You're not going to make any spelling errors that you can't fix later, so you don't need it. And if you carry it with you "just in case," you will use it. One minute you'll be fixing punctuation, the next minute that whole chapter about the neighbor's lawn will be one big white smear.

3) Give yourself, and your tired writing hand, a break. If you start to run low on ideas, stop writing and let your mind and hands recharge at the same time. If you're having a burst of inspiration that's driving you to write for hours, force yourself to take breaks when you come to the end of a chapter or the top of the hour.

4) Don't worry about adding each line to your word count as you write it. Instead, count when you stop for the day, or when you pause to give your writing hand a break. Write your updated word count at the top of your last written page, so that you can easily locate it when you tally up your next section.

5) Don't buy expensive pens to novel with. Ten thousand words later, your pen will start to run out of ink, and you'll be $7 in the hole. Go for a pack of inexpensive (but not dollar-store) pens with blue or black permanent ink. Avoid erasable ink, as you'll be tempted to make edits—even if you have a will of iron. For the same reasons, don't novel longhand in pencil.

Reintroducing Yourself to the World as a Novelist

One fringe benefit of writing a book is being seen by those around you in the new, vastly sexier light of your novelist status. Displaying your new writer self may feel uncomfortable at first, but give it a try. Social gatherings are a great place to practice the brilliant self-absorption that you'll need to emanate as a novelist.

Maximizing the benefits of a party situation is a learned skill, and it can be difficult for novice writers, especially as the party wears on and the patrons become increasingly drunk and prone to talking about all manner of things, most of which are unrelated to your novel.

Steering every conversation back to your book isn't impossible, though. It just requires a certain amount of conversational finesse. Witness the following model tête-à-tête:

Writer: So, what's up, partygoer?

Partygoer: Not much! I've been pretty sick lately with that flu that's been going around, so I've just been laying low. Sleeping a lot. You know . . .

Writer: Oh, man! That's so funny you would say that. The protagonist in my novel had this moment where he thought about opening an office supply store that sold only wiener dogs.

THOUGHTS FROM THE TRENCHES: NANOWRIMO WINNERS ON "THE END"

"When Week Four shows up, I grit my teeth. This is when I'm typically close to fifty thousand words, but miles away from the end of the story. I bring out the broadest brush in my arsenal. Entire scenes get described in a few sentences as I rush to begin detailing the plot elements necessary for the story. I race to build to the climax. For the past two years, I've been forced to write twenty thousand words in two or three days to get the story on paper. I find the exhilaration of typing "The End" to be so intense, so moving, that I typically cry as I type those words."
—Russell Kremer, 51, three-time NaNoWriMo winner from Los Angeles

"The best thing about Week Four is coming to the end of the book. The worst thing about Week Four is coming to the end of the

book and realizing that I am short eight thousand words, and that I have to add an entire additional subplot, or change the ending, something, anything, to hit 50,000 words. I hit this point in my second book and was bemoaning it at the dinner table, and my husband said, "You need to kill somebody. That should be good for eight thousand words." So I did. I killed the protagonist's husband."
—Rise Sheridan-Peters, 42, three-time NaNoWriMo winner from Washington, D.C.

"There's a lot of giggling to yourself, partially because by this point you've become slightly mad, but I think also because you're free to really take yourself less seriously."
—Ryan Dunsmuir, 38, five-time NaNoWriMo winner from Brooklyn

Partygoer (laughing): What a brilliant plot idea! I feel better already!

Writer: Yeah. Cracked me up, too. But he didn't end up doing it. Maybe in the sequel, huh?

Partygoer (getting out a pen): I need your autograph right now.

Another key point to remember—whether developing your sterling literary reputation at social gatherings or one on one—is that the novel you just completed is *not* your first novel. Even if it is, in fact, your first novel. In all conversations, you should refer to your manuscript as "my most recent novel."

Technically speaking, this is accurate. And it also implies the existence of a host of other, earlier novels whose existence you are humble enough not to get into at that moment. In the unlikely situation that someone asks for a synopsis of your earlier novels, say your agent has asked you not to talk about them. Then roll your eyes, shrug your shoulders, and sigh, "The *publishing* world . . ."

A LETTER

For you to read upon reaching 50,000 words. Or at the end of the month, whichever comes first.

Congratulations!

Dear Novelist,

It is my pleasure to inform you that you have officially kicked ass this month.

No matter how many words you have written, you have done an amazing thing. Through distractions and demands and family obligations, you forged ahead. Your willingness to go out on a creative limb, to stand up and reach for an impossible goal, is an inspiring example to all of us.

For those of you who managed to write 50,000 words this month, know that writing so much so quickly is a task that most professional writers would run from screaming. You have eaten the challenge for breakfast, and cleaned your teeth with its footnotes. You are brave, talented, and brimming with the kind of loquacious storytelling skill that no doubt will serve you well in your new job as up-and-coming novelist.

NO PLOT? NO PROBLEM!

And if you fell a little short of 50,000 but still wrote your heart out, I have a little secret to share: In the course of this great experiment in caffeine consumption, the goal of 50,000 words has been, shall we say, overemphasized. One of the things month-long noveling does is get your sense of scale all out of whack. This is done intentionally, because anyone with a realistic sense of perspective wouldn't try to write a novel in a month.

As the month ends, though, I feel it is my ethical responsibility to bring some perspective back into your life. So listen closely: If you "only" wrote 15,000 words over the past four weeks, you invented fifty (that's 50, five-oh) book pages of fiction. Those of you who made it to the 25,000-word point wrote eighty-three pages. In a month. *Hello?*

This is something to write home about.

And in this letter home, you should include a few things. One of them being the fact that you chose to try. This may seem like a little thing—this trying—but it is not. You put your name out there for the world to see. You risked failure. And just by risking failure, you avoided it entirely.

Let me explain. You could have spent this month living your normal life. You could have gone for long walks with your lover or won points with your boss by coming into work without those big bags under your eyes. Instead you agreed to do something dumb. You agreed to try and write more fiction than you ever have in a month.

Most of you—like me—probably do not write fiction. Fiction is something other people write. But this month, you dared to say, "Screw that. It's my turn." You stepped up to the plate. And there is nothing more admirable in this whole damn world than someone willing to set for themselves the fearsome task of trying something big.

So be proud, writer. You've done something fantastic this month, and I salute you for it.

Now please do me a favor and go grab those bottles of champagne (or suitable champagne substitute) you bought in chapter eight. One of the bottles is for you. And the other is a gift for you to present to your MVPs: the friends and family who helped you get through this tumultuous month.

And as you gather with your loved ones to celebrate your achievements and the end of a crazy, productive month, please accept my congratulations and a toast. To you and all you've done. And to the joyful power of dreams realized.

CHAPTER 9

I Wrote
a Novel.
Now What?

It's been a month of stress and jubilation, panic and triumph. And now, somehow, it's over.

After all the frenzied productivity and endorphin-spraying bursts of creative accomplishment, you'll likely find your return to normal life a little . . . weird. Truman Capote famously compared finishing a book to taking a favorite child outside and shooting him. While your book is still a few steps away from being finished, you *have* completed a huge portion of it, and you will be feeling the tingles of loss, emptiness, and powder burn that Capote described in the coming weeks.

NaNoWriMo participants refer to this feeling of aimlessness as the "post-NaNo Blues" or "postnovel depression." Whatever it's called, I've come down with a huge case of it each of the five years I've written a novel. At the close of Week Four, I feel like I'm being wrenched awake from a beautiful, crazy dream. I don't know what to do with myself, and all I want is to burrow back down into the warm depths and reconnect with the stories zipping around my head.

But as soon as the deadline lifts, my connection to that fantasy world is lost, and the real world comes rushing in. As you come down off your writer's high this week, you too will be deluged with an array of chores and errands; the everyday must-dos that you've been so rightly putting off for the past month to focus on your writing.

Your immediate instinct when faced with such a bewildering array of stimulus may be similar to mine: to retreat into your novel; to block out the world and burrow back into the comfortably snug confines of your fictional world.

Don't do it.

Despite what you may have learned last month, sustained writing is best accomplished as part of a balanced lifestyle, one that includes things like grocery shopping and speaking in complete sentences with your significant other. No matter how dreadful it seems, you should take a vacation from your novel, for at least a couple of weeks, to get some balance back in your life and to get some perspective on what you just wrote.

Trust me: The novel is going to be right there waiting for you when you get back. Right now, your friends, family, and creditors are calling. Spend the coming month getting reacquainted with the essential distractions that you successfully avoided during the last one.

And when all of that is done, when calm has been regained, when you've gotten a little objective distance from your manuscript, then you will be ready for the next awesome experience: reading it.

TURNING THE PAGES AND MAKING THE CALL

After some well-deserved R&R, make a date with your novel. Set aside an entire evening for just the two of you. No phone calls, no visitors, and no red pens to catch spelling mistakes. You're going to spend a couple of hours just getting reacquainted with your book.

Chances are, in reading over the manuscript, you'll be pleasantly surprised. It won't be that bad at all, especially for a month's labors. Then, when you've finished reading it, first page to last, ask yourself the following question: Do I want to devote a year of my life to making it better?

The answer may be no. And that's an okay answer. *No Plot? No Problem!* is as much a guide to recharging your imagination as it is a path toward book production. With our busy lives, we have to pick

 GETTING A SECOND OPINION

Having someone else critique your novel can bo either immensely helpful or a discouraging waste of time, depending on who you ask. If you'd like a second opinion on what works and what doesn't in your book before you start the rewrite, here are some tips to keep in mind:

Choose someone whose literary tastes are similar to yours. This is absolutely essential. Yes, good stories transcend genre. But at this stage in the game, you want to put your book in the hands of someone who understands and loves the kind of story you wrote. Not only will the person better appreciate and enjoy your book, his or her critique will be more knowledgeable and appropriate to what you need.

Choose a tactful, diplomatic reader. Even the thickest-skinned writer is going to be shaking when it comes time to hear The Verdict from a reader. Choose someone you trust to be both honest *and* kind. You don't want your first review to leave you wanting to abandon writing forever.

Tell the person what you want critiqued. Should the reader look for typos? Clichés? Big-picture things? Are you worried that your dialogue sounds stilted? Let your reader know exactly what you want his or her opinion on, so you get the right feedback.

Listen. Then, when The Verdict comes, listen, take notes, and stifle your impulse to argue or explain anything. Just ask as many questions as you can, and try to get your reader to talk as much as possible about everything in the book, from the chapter lengths to his or her favorite scenes.

our battles, and there's every chance that you just won't like the book you wrote enough to wrangle it into shape.

Two of the five novels I've written fit into this category. The first time it happened, I was devastated. It was my second NaNoWriMo, and I made the mistake I describe in chapter two, one common amongst second-year participants: I got overly ambitious with my characters, and I allowed all sorts of depressing nonsense from my Magna Carta II list to sneak in.

The next year, I thought I had learned my lesson, but once again I waded knee-deep into the trough of failure. This time I kept the characters on such a tight rein that the book ended up feeling claustrophobic and overwritten, plagued with a lack of action and a jaw-dropping amount of filler.

With back-to-back noveling failures to my credit, "exuberant imperfection" started seeming less like a panic-free way to get monumental tasks accomplished and more like a surefire way to make me feel like a moron. Not caring if I wrote crap and stumbling into passable prose was exhilarating. Not caring if I wrote crap and getting exactly that for two years in a row was demoralizing.

Just as I was about to drop my laptop into a trash compactor, though, a friend of mine sent me some quotes from the celebrated graphic designer Bruce Mau. One of which struck pretty close to home.

 CREATING A NOVEL BLOOPERS FILE

Just as one of the first things you did when you started writing was to create a "Novel Notes" file on your computer, so should you now create a "Novel Cuts" file. Use this as the home for every deletion longer than a couple of sentences. You might change your mind about that deleted scene later, and you'll also want to have the unexpurgated version of the book on hand when the biographers come sniffing around your estate in a couple of decades.

"Love your experiments (as you would an ugly child)," Mau's maxim went. "Exploit the liberty in casting your work as beautiful experiments, iterations, attempts, trials, and errors. Take the long view and allow yourself the fun of failure every day."

As corny as it sounds, those words changed the way I looked at my two crapulent works of fiction. As literature, they were ugly as sin. As experiments, though, they were packed with a beautiful, useful array of wrong turns, misguided decisions, and shameful flops. From those experiments, I discovered copious amounts about what I *shouldn't* be writing. This allowed me to spend my fourth and fifth novels in the happy pursuit of what I should.

Inspiration and insight, I've learned, flow more freely from failures than they do from successes. Even if your novel is beyond editorial salvation, your imagination has gotten a great work out, and you'll likely have a much easier time on whatever creative challenge you tackle next.

And if your answer is yes, you would like to revise your manuscript to perfection—well, roll up those sleeves and read on.

WHITTLING THE STUMP:
THE KNOTTY ISSUES OF REWRITING

Rewriting is when your novel—the version that people will fight one another for in bookstores—is born. What you spent the last thirty days creating amounts to a large, knotty wooden stump. It's a powerful, brute object, and it's absolutely amazing that you conjured such a dense mass out of thin air. But it's also likely too unwieldy at this point to take outside the home.

In the editing process, that stump will get whittled into a lithe, diabolical instrument that will eventually leave literary agents clutching their hearts in fear and wonder.

Making the myriad tweaks, fixes, and alterations necessary to get your book up to bookstore quality is a huge, challenging project.

When you realize that most novels on the bookstore shelf were not rewritten once but numerous times, you will begin to see why even the youngest professional novelists have the skittish, prematurely aged appearance of people who have endured a lifetime of unspeakable tragedies.

The good news, though, is that the difficulties of rewriting are absolutely worth it, and that taking your novel from the rough draft stage to the shining, breathtaking end product will delight and devastate you just as intensely as the rough draft did, if not more so.

TRADING CHAINSAWS FOR DENTAL PICKS (AND THE RETURN OF A FAMILIAR SECRET WEAPON)

In my experience, the basic key to editing is this: Slow down. This is especially true for those of us who spent a month writing their rough draft at literary Warp Factor Ninety. If you attack your second draft with the same reckless zeal that you used to such triumphant effect on your first draft, you'll end up hurtling right past almost all of the fine-tunings and microadjustments that your second draft needs.

This reduced pace will feel excruciating at first, especially because you know you have so much ground to cover. But by its nature it's painstaking, brow-furrowing work, and it's meant to be taken one page at a time. The days of the chainsaw are over; from here on out, we'll be using small, diamond blades and dental picks.

Oh, and a secret weapon.

Unlike the devilish device you met in chapter one—the deadline—this writing aid is actually an old acquaintance of yours. One we've been keeping locked up in our kennels for the past month.

Yes, your Inner Editor is ready to come home.

I know, I know: This is not the greatest news. You've been doing just fine without all the nit-picking, second-guessing, and perfectionist carping that you've come to expect from your Inner Editor.

A WRITER, RECHARGED, BY GAYLE BRANDEIS

I had always been an in-the-flow writer. I could sit down and let the words pour. Then, in 2002, I became an "author." The transition from being a writer who blissfully gushed words to being a published author with a sudden awareness of audience was more complicated than I had anticipated. It was a wonderful and gratifying transition, but I also felt the new weight of expectation, the pressures of a fickle market. It took some of the joy out of my process. I began to feel more self-conscious, more blocked, as I wrote. My first book was *Fruitflesh: Seeds of Inspiration for Women Who Write*. It felt kind of ironic to be talking to people about the juiciness of writing when my own writing life was drier than it had ever been.

While I was on my book tour, I found out that my novel, *The Book of Dead Birds*, had won Barbara Kingsolver's Bellwether Prize for Fiction and would be published the following year by HarperCollins. While this news was beyond thrilling, it served to hamper my natural creative flow even more. How could my work live up to such accolades?

Then a friend told me about NaNoWriMo. I figured it was worth a shot—I thought that if I forced myself to write something that fast, it would be liberating; I wouldn't have time to worry about how good my work was, wouldn't have to worry about anyone peering over my shoulder. And that's exactly what happened. Plowing forward

blindly loosened me up. Writing became fun and free-flowing again. And my beloved characters from *The Book of Dead Birds* started speaking to me again. The work that was born that November recharged me like an electric shock.

When I was on tour for *The Book of Dead Birds*, my mother-in-law's husband, Jack, was diagnosed with brain cancer, and I flew home early to be with the family. On the plane, I was feeling too upset to talk with anyone, but the woman next to me cajoled me into conversation. She had just lost a brother to brain cancer, so we had a lot to talk about. She also mentioned that she went to auctions at self-storage places and sold her winnings at yard sales. I had never heard of such a practice, and I found myself intrigued. Sadly, Jack died the following week. We were still deep in mourning by the time November rolled around. I couldn't stop thinking about the woman on the plane and her stories of self-storage auctions, so I decided to use that as the seed for my 2003 NaNoWriMo endeavor. I felt Jack's presence in every word I wrote.

I am happy to say that the resulting novel, *Self Storage*, is going to be published by Ballantine in 2007 as part of a two-book deal. Of course, I dedicated the book to Jack. Not only did NaNoWriMo bring my writing back to life; it is helping me keep the memory of a wonderful man alive as well.

However, only your Inner Editor can help you spot all the improvements your novel needs. And besides, your Inner Editor's stay in the kennel has done it a world of good. It's mellowed and tanned; it's become, dare I say it, a kinder, gentler Inner Editor. Frankly, I think you doing such fantastic work without its help has humbled it a little bit.

So the caustic, biting days are over. From here on out, the criticism will be (mostly) constructive, and I think you two would make an excellent team on this upcoming project.

So you ready to have it back?

GIVE ME BACK MY INNER EDITOR

Just touch the button, and it's yours.

Now let's dive into that rewrite.

THE BIG PICTURE: FINDING YOUR STORY ARC

First, grab your printout and a nice, friendly pen. Choose a color other than red, like purple or green. Now read each chapter in order and, in the margins at the start of each one, jot down the following:

1) The characters who appear

2) The action that occurs

Some examples of these margin notes might be: "Chapter Two: This is where we meet Phil, the main love interest, in all his idiotic glory, and where we learn that Amy is unhappy with her imminent arranged marriage to Thaddeus Morgenheimer, King of the Orangutans."

Or: "Chapter Four: This is where the protagonist learns, through the mandatory drug screening at the Pizza Hut, that Bill has a rare form of leprosy, and he gets the idea that he can enlist the aid of a late-night TV psychic to cure himself."

What you are doing with this review is clarifying your novel's current structure, to see how your book's interrelated plots and subplots play out across the chapters. As you take your inventory of your characters and their actions, you should do so with the cold, dispassionate eye of a mechanic seeing a prototype car for the first time. At this point, all you're trying to do is understand how the machine works; improving the performance of the engine, and adding the all-important racing stripes and fender detailing, will come later.

**HOW I EDITED MY MONTH-LONG MANUSCRIPT
INTO A TWO-BOOK DEAL WITH WARNER BOOKS,
BY LANI DIANE RICH**

I wrote my first book, *Time Off for Good Behavior*, during NaNoWriMo 2002. A group of writer friends were doing it, and in the grand tradition of jumping off a bridge if your friends are doing it, I went along. By November 25th, I had written a 50,005-word novel (what can I say, I'm not an overachiever), and it became my holiday party icebreaker: "Hey, dig me, I wrote a *novel*."

The thing about having a finished novel lying around the house is that it gets you thinking about selling it. At that point, I was home with the kids and keeping sane by writing during every spare moment anyway, so I decided to give professional writing a shot. I revised *Time Off* and sent it out to friends for comments. As luck would have it, I got lucky. Someone who'd read my first chapter recommended me to her agent. The agent loved it and signed me—wahoo! She submitted my book, and six weeks later, I

had a two-book contract with Warner. To top it all off, in July 2005 *Time Off for Good Behavior* took the coveted RITA award for Best First Book, surprising no one more than me! So don't let anyone tell you it can't be done, because they'd be full of crap.

Now, true, I'm a bit of a freak in the book business. Typically, people spend years trying to get their novels published; I hit on some lightning speed mojo. But forget the timeline and look at the result; it *can* happen. Since then, I've contracted a total of six books between two publishers (*Maybe Baby*, released by Warner Forever in June 2005, also started out as a NaNoWriMo book), and if I can do it, so can you. The important thing is that you write, and that you give yourself permission to write crap, if necessary. Crap you can edit. A blank page will never be anything but. God bless, and get writing!

Laying Out the Cards

When you're done with your chapter-by-chapter analysis, the arc of your story will be laid bare, a fact that will either be exciting or depressing, depending on how cohesive your story turned out. No matter how tight the tale, though, there is still plenty of room for improvement. Which is what we'll do now.

Let's start by transposing your story into movable outline form. I like to use four-by-six-inch note cards for this, but you can also do it digitally using Power Point presentation slides, cells on a spreadsheet, or any other tool that allows you to transpose bits of information easily.

Now, break down each chapter into its component scenes, and create an index card (or Power Point slide, etc.) for each scene, noting the same information you did for the chapter-by-chapter analysis—the cast, the action, and what role the scene plays in advancing the storyline of the book.

After you've made a card for each scene, lay the cards out in the order they appear in your book. Use a vertical divider (I like pencils) to group the cards into chapters. Then step back and marvel: There it is, your month's labors laid out in a long line of action/reaction, a book's worth of plot and story sailing in a straight line across the floor of your apartment or desktop.

Cutting the Cards

Here's where we take apart and rebuild your book's engine. As you look at the story, you'll likely find that you have many random digressions and out-of-left-field tangents. In the rough draft phase, these were vibrant labs for the production of new ideas and angles. And let's face it: They were also easy ways to amass the day's word-count quota.

There's no shame in that. Now, though, you need to decide what really belongs in your book. As you scan your cards, remove the obvious filler scenes and set them aside. If you're not sure whether a scene is essential or not, leave it in for now.

Next, look at your remaining cast of characters. Chances are good that in writing your rough draft you introduced more people than your story has room to accommodate. Some of these superfluous voices are simply doubles of other characters, and others may be evolutionary vestiges of earlier, discarded story directions.

As you view your story from above, ask yourself if all of the characters have a reason for being there. Do they end up advancing the story in some way? If not, trim, slice, and winnow. Don't be too overzealous with the knife, however: In your character paring, you may find a pointless but absolutely lovable stowaway who you're reluctant to evict from your tale. If so, think about crafting a new relationship or twist that might bind the person more tightly to the core of your story. If necessary, create new index cards to serve as placeholding reminders of any new scenes you'll need to write.

Once your roll-call of characters is set, consider whether each one is developed properly; there are probably some you need to spend more time with. As mentioned in chapter five, balanced "camera time" for each character is crucial, especially if you've written the story in third-person or are telling your novel through multiple points of view.

If you do have multiple protagonists, think about the "through-lines" of each character. Do you tell each character's story in multi-chapter blocks? If so, maybe switching to a different character every chapter (or within chapters) might give your novel more energy.

Shuffling the Cards

Which brings us to the next phase of the "big picture" rewrite: figuring out your book's pacing. After you've trimmed all the obvious fat and have what seem to be all the essential pieces, it's time to address questions of flow, tension, and payoff.

HOW LONG DOES A REWRITE USUALLY TAKE?

Rewrites vary, of course, but a year is a pretty good estimate. If you're absolutely fanatical about it and can spend every weekend revising, you may be able to do it in half that. Taking a novel-editing class is one option, as is signing up for the free National Novel Editing Month (www.nanoedmo.org). Run by NaNoWriMo veteran Lauren Ayer, NaNoEdMo gives writers a mission and a deadline: pounding out fifty hours of rewriting in the month of March.

This is the beauty of using cards, since you can literally shuffle them, taking the story apart and putting it back together in any number of alternate ways. Do this deliberately now, testing different structures and ideas, until you have a gorgeous, surprising, yet inevitable-seeming arc for your story. You may find more pieces to cut or holes that need filling. If you're at a loss over the best way to organize the book, move the cards at random, purposefully throwing everything out of whack. Sometimes a seemingly haphazard alignment can open up new through-lines in your story, bringing a sweet, soaring readability to a book that used to trudge along.

Here are some questions you might ask yourself as you shuffle the deck: Does it seem like the story gets off to a dynamic start at the beginning, only to lose steam at the end? Or do the opening chapters have too much exposition and not enough action? When it comes to the story's timeline, do you take a direct, chronological approach to your book? Or do you use flashbacks and reminiscences to jog the story back and forth from present to past? How might you shuffle scenes to heighten the story's drama, comedy, or suspense?

Once you've come up with a winning order for your scenes, implement those changes in your manuscript. Cut and paste the scenes into the right sequence, but as much as possible avoid rewriting; if you have new scenes you need to write, use descriptive placeholders for the moment. Until all your book's pieces are in place, you don't want to get bogged down in minutiae.

THE SMALL PICTURE: POLISHING YOUR PROSE

Now we break out the dental picks and, in a separate revision step, make the sentence-by-sentence, word-by-word changes that will clean and polish your story so it sparkles. This is the phase that will take you a long, long time. And though the tweaks each novel requires will vary, there are a few small-picture messes particular to month-long novels.

The first of these is wooden prose. As you read through your book, you may be a little surprised at the starkness of the language. Rushed, utilitarian descriptions and atrociously stiff dialogue are both side effects of writing so much, so quickly.

In your rewrite, you have the wonderful opportunity to decorate your book with the kind of delicious linguistic flourishes that are inevitably lacking in a first draft. As you revise, be sure to vary your sentence lengths, and keep your descriptors vibrant. Watch for pat adjectives and similes like "ice-blue" eyes or minds that function "like steel traps." If your seas are roiling and bosoms heaving, you should spend a little of your copious amount of editing time coming up with fresher, more accurate descriptions.

Your characters' conversations also likely suffered from the rush job. Look closely at every instance someone speaks: Is the language natural, realistic, and true to the character? I know that the loquaciousness of my characters corresponds directly with the amount I was behind on the week's word-count quota. Examine the content of dialogue, and ask yourself if each conversation is necessary to move the story forward or to help reveal the characters. If not, rewrite or cut them.

The other easily correctable, oft-seen problem with month-long novels concerns the props and cultural ephemera used in the background of the story. As you sketched your novel's scenery, you likely grabbed whatever materials were convenient at the time. Your protagonist may have been singing along to the songs playing on the radio as you wrote, and may have had long discussions about movies you'd recently seen or books you'd just read.

Often times, these haphazard background elements will fit surprisingly well with your story. But during the editing process you should look skeptically at all these details and flourishes, particularly those that you copied and pasted from life around you. References to songs, movies, and other pieces of popular culture are all excellent ways to add layers of meaning into a novel, but when used sloppily, they tend to be more puzzling than powerful.

In the editing process, you'll also need to do those tiresome research and accuracy checks you wisely skipped when writing your rough draft. Do you have the rainy season sweeping through your Indonesian novel in the proper months? Do Finnish people really eat their weight in cupcakes every year? Where *is* Saskatoon, anyway? The Internet likely has the answers to all your pressing fact-checking problems.

LITERARY AGENT ARIELLE ECKSTUT ON LANDING THE RIGHT AGENT FOR YOUR BOOK

So you're done with your rewrite and ready to land an agent. Great! I asked Arielle Eckstut, an agent for Levine-Greenberg, a New York literary agency, and the coauthor of *Putting Your Passion into Print*, to offer her advice on sending your book out into the agent-o-sphere.

Rule 1: Don't send a rough draft. Before you send your manuscript to an agent, make sure you've done everything you possibly can to make it the very best it can be. In fact, it's ideal to have a number of people read and comment on your manuscript before you send it off because there's simply no way to have the kind of objectivity you need on your own. The best kinds of readers are those who would actually buy your book in a bookstore. If you've written a sci-fi thriller and your wife only reads nineteenth-century British fiction, look for advice outside the home!

Rule 2: Don't send your manuscript to random agents. Much like finding readers, you'll want to find an agent who represents books like yours. To find this kind of agent, look in the acknowledgments section of books that are similar in voice, content, and spirit as yours. Authors often thank their agents in the acknowledgments. Once you've found at least a dozen agents, research them. Search the Web, or look them up in Jeff

Herman's *The Writer's Guide to Book Editors, Publishers, and Literary Agents*. See which ones feel like a potential match. Then, when you write your query letters, let them know why you think they're a good match and how your book fits in with the rest of their list.

Rule 3: Submit your query letter to multiple agents simultaneously. Otherwise, you could wait twenty-five years before you find an agent (see Rule 5). Note: Do *not* send the manuscript with your query letter. Wait until the agent requests it. The only exception to this rule is if you're querying an agent by email. In this case, you can attach the manuscript (or the first couple of chapters) as a Word document. If you're wondering why, it's because email attachments take up no room on the agent's already overcrowded desk!

Rule 4: God is in the details. Make sure everything is neatly packaged. If it's a big manuscript, put it in a nice stationery box. Put *all* your contact information in your query letter and on the cover page of your novel. Make sure to put the title, your name, and the page number in a header or footer on every page. Make sure your manuscript is double-spaced, single-sided, and unbound. Run a spell check. Look for odd page breaks. If you're not detail oriented, find someone who is to do a careful check of everything before you send it off.

Rule 5: Be patient. It's not unheard of for an agent to take a year—that's right, a year—to get back to a writer about his or her query or manuscript. So there's a lot of waiting involved when finding an agent. And, remember, just because you're not hearing anything doesn't mean bad news. On the other hand, don't be afraid to follow up, especially if an agent has requested your materials. A friendly, biweekly call is perfectly appropriate.

A FINAL WORD ON GETTING PUBLISHED

Whenever I talk about all the big picture and microscopic changes a revision requires, I frequently hear the following lament from NaNoWriMo participants: "The book market is so tight, and I probably don't stand a chance in hell of getting published. So why should I waste my time on a rewrite?"

When faced with this question, I think of my friend Brent. Brent is an engineer, and his weekdays are filled with incredibly complex mathematical equations and indecipherable codes.

On weekends, Brent plays softball.

Now, Brent is not the greatest softball player. Brent played volley-ball in college on his school's team, and he's a slamming, spiking terror at the net. He's also a force to be reckoned with on the basket-ball court.

On the softball diamond, though, Brent has a lot to learn. Which is partly why he does it. To challenge himself. To grow. The pitchers of beer after the game don't hurt either.

Anyway, whenever people express their reluctance to invest time in something that won't have proven results, I ask them what *they* do for fun on weekends.

Invariably, the time they spend running around on basketball courts, rearranging Scrabble tiles, or slaying video game monsters is not done in an effort to make millions of dollars from corporate sponsorships. Or because they think it will make them famous.

No. They do it because the challenge of the game simply feels good. They do it because they like to compete, because they like spending time with friends, because it feels really, really nice to just lose themselves in the visceral pleasure of an activity.

Novel-writing is just a recreational sport where you don't have to get up out of your chair. And that's exactly how I encourage writers to approach revisions. As you edit, do it in the spirit of a playground softball game. No stakes, no pressure. No one in the stands watching or judging. Just you versus a dozen easily distracted, unathletic third-graders who will believe anything you say about outs and ups because they think you're the gym teacher.

Okay, forget that part about the third-graders. But you know what I'm saying. Don't waste your time thinking about the agents, the publishers, or the market. It's just you, and it's just for fun. And, should things go well, you'll have a convenient paper record of your heroic deeds to share for decades to come.

But even if this book doesn't pan out, there's always the next one. And the one after that. So go for it. Swing hard; take risks; aim for the bleachers. The game begins anew every day, and it only gets better from here.

Acknowledgments

Thanks, firstly, to all the National Novel Writing Month staff, participants, and Municipal Liaisons. You make NaNoWriMo an incredible place to be every November.

I'd also like to thank my powerhouse editorial team of Leslie Jonath and Jeff Campbell. Your encouragement, support, and grammatical know-how have meant the world to me.

A tall high-five as well to Arielle Eckstut, agent extraordinaire, for setting all of this in motion, and for being such a patient, enthusiatic guide to the publishing world.

Much gratitude to the NaNoWriMo participants and supporters who have been absolutely essential in the creation of this book. These heroes and heroines include: Tim Lohnes, Dan Strachota, Brent Searcy, Kathleen Dodge, Rolf Nelson, Michelle Smith, Wendy Smith, Michele Posner, Kristina Malsberger, Victoria Schlesinger, Lauren Ayer, Erin Allday, Matt Nelson, Trena Taylor, Rich Thomas, Ed Chang, Lisa Eckstein, Amy Probst, Jodi Brandon, Sharon Voon, Suzy Rogers, Kara Platoni, Kara Akins, Jennifer McCreedy, Russell Kremer, Irfon Ahmad, Jennifer Bryant, Sand Pilarski, Fiona Juan, Mark Swarthout, Laurie Jackson, Michael Cieslak, Andrew Johnson, Alexandra Queen, Denise Roe, Brian Baldi, Ryan Dunsmuir, Carolyn Lawrence, Kimberli Munkres, Laura Hastings, Michele Marques, Cybele May, Stacy Katz, Carol McBay, Lani Diane Rich, Michael Sirois, Feath MacKirin, Ian Dudley, Rachel Young, Amy Eason, Elke Sisco, Tedi Trindle, Dan Laci, Benj Vardigan, Ann Kasunich, Ysabet MacFarlane, Julia Cardis, Tom Mannarelli, Russ Uman, Amy Lombardi, Andy Greenwald, Dan Sanderson, Gayle Brandeis, Diane Reese, Michele Booher, Patrick Vilain, Jennifer Herbinson, James Shields, Eric Doherty, Alicia Bergin, Calla Devlin, and Brenda Tucker.

Last and decidedly not least, I owe enormous, never-ending, gobstopping thanks to Elly Karl, who, should they ever try to make a movie of this book, will have to play the roles of girlfriend, coach, cheerleader, chef, and patron saint simultaneously.

Index